□ □ □ □ □ □ □ □ □ □ □ □ □ □ □ □ □

IN-HOUSE TEAM

Editor: Mike Toller

Features editor: Alexi Duggins

Senior editorial assistant: Joly Braime

Editorial and production assistant: Alix Fox

Editorial assistance: Anton Tweedale, Claire Gardiner, Kelsey Strand-Polyak, Katy Georgiou

Designer: Sarah Winter

Design assistance: Caitlin Kenney, Sara Gramner

Picture research: Alex Amend

Production consultant: Iain Leslie

Web editor: Cameron J Macphail

National ad sales: Sue Ostler, Zee Ahmad

Distribution: Nativeps

Financial controller: Sharon Evans

Managing director: Ian Merricks

Publisher: Itchy Group

Cover illustration: Si Clark (www.si-clark.co.uk)

© 2007 Itchy Group

ISBN: 978-1-905705-21-4

Andrew Hoskins, Kerrie Fuller, Karl Williams, Rachel Bull, Pamela Jones, Joanna Lester, Katy Georgiou, Anna Addison, Ellen Godwin, Samuel Munch-Petersen, Jon Bines, Sarah B, Andy Whitehead, Lucy Titterington, Katie Spain

Photography: Ben Gilbert, Helen Kennedy, Bas Driessen, GJ Blues, Claudia Black, Dorrottya Verses, Nicky Tiney, Becky Wicks, Tim Ireland, Tara Hill, Chris Grossmeier, Emily Payne, Selma Yalazi Dawani, Carl Ratcliff, Sarah Morecombe James Maskrey, Maira Kouvara, Mario Alberto

Illustrations: Tom Denbigh, Si Clark, Joly Braime

Itchy Group, White Horse Yard
78 Liverpool Road, London, N1 0QD
Tel: 020 7288 9810 **Fax:** 020 7288 9815
E-mail: editor@itchymedia.co.uk
Web: www.itchycity.co.uk

□□□□□□□□□□□□□□□□□□

Welcome to Itchy 2007

You lucky thing, you. Whether you've bought, borrowed, begged or pinched it off your best mate's bookshelf, you've managed to get your mucky paddles on an Itchy guide. And what a guide it is. If you're a regular reader, you're probably already impressing your friends with your dazzling knowledge of where to head for a rip-roaring time. If, on the other hand, you're a trembling Itchy virgin, then get ready to live life as you've never lived it before. We've spent the last year scouring London for the very best places to booze, cruise, schmooze, snooze and lose ourselves to the forces of pleasure. As ever, we've made the necessary, erm, sacrifices in the name of our research – dancing nights away, shopping 'til we flop and of course, eating and drinking more than we ever thought possible. But we're still alive, and now we're ready to do the whole lot again. Come with us if you're up for it – the first round's on us...

KEY TO SYMBOLS

🕐 Opening times

🍽 Itchy's favourite dish

🍷 Cost of a bottle of house wine

🎟 Admission price

Welcome to London

A Frenchman once said to us 'a man 'oo taahres of Lernden, taahres of laahfe'. Once we worked out what the hell he was saying, we found this quite amusing, not only because he'd tried to pass off this famous quote as his own, but also because he farted as he said it. He had this look of dented pride, much like when a cat falls off a fence and looks at you with complete horror, before recovering their composure into an 'I meant to do that' face.

Regardless of our froggy friend's penchant for plagiarism, he really meant what he said, and providing you're up for making the most of London's quirks, he was bang on the money.

The Big Smoke's long and alluringly twisted (in both senses) history makes for some unique and mind-bending experiences. One minute you're in Jack the Ripper's seedy Victorian London, walking down foggy Clink Street in London Bridge (home of the infamous prison), then suddenly you're in wartime London, listening to a beautiful pianist playing Vera Lynn songs by the river, and before you can say 'jellied eels' you're in some groovy bar, swinging as hard as they did in the sixties.

It's true that London has a seemingly inexhaustible catalogue of pubs, bars, clubs, restaurants, galleries, museums and shops, but there's so much more than the drunken bright lights and wallet-bothering consumer traps; all you have to do is look a little harder. There are countless freebie adventures to experience in this town; London has acres of parks to ramble through, scores of fascinating buildings to explore and hidden areas of outstandingly inspiring beauty.

Itchy is here to provide you with the inside track; to help guide you through the splendid, sprawling mess of culture that courses through London's infinite veins. Our veritable army of fun-seeking reprobates have an unparalleled collective knowledge of London's over and underground delights.

From a belly-pleasing Brick Lane salt beef sandwich to the implausible winter beach parties of the South Bank, there's not a gum-encrusted paving stone we've left unturned in our quest to show you how to live this city to the full (as you might expect, considering that we even braved a flatulent Frenchie in the name of research). Now take a read. We promise that unlike us, you'll wind up smelling of roses.

Introduction

Two hours in London

Footloose, fancy-free and after something to do to kill a couple of hours? Then it's time to check out some real London authenticity. And we're not talking about hanging out in some grotty boozer. A number of the capital's pubs might have been there since 1870, but there's more to 'real London' than an ancient fag-stained carpet. Our fave way to kill time's a trip east to Columbia Road Flower Market – it's bloomin' marvellous.

You'll find over 50 stalls crammed onto a narrow street in the East End every Saturday, selling quality, weird and wacky green stuff (of the legal kind).

Since the 19th century Londoners have flocked here to load up on floral fancies, and the bric-a-brac shops that surround it never fail to take us back in time; as do the old-school caffs with the cheery, fag-in-mouth hospitality of their grammatically-challenged employees.

The same street on a Sunday is sadly not the same, but a modern twist sees nearby Spitalfields bustling with fashion fanatics and foodies. And if wandering amongst all the daffodils has left you feeling lonely as a cloud, head to the bars along Brick Lane. There aren't so many flowers on offer, but you'll certainly find a few people willing to sow their seeds.

Two days in London

You've got two whole days to spend exploring and you're determined to do something new that doesn't involve straying too far into the darkened, barren wasteland of your overdraft. Your momma might have told you'd there'd be days like these, but what she probably didn't think to tell you is that when you're after pays like these, South of the river's where it's at. For cheapo days out with a difference we always head dahn Saarf.

Before you venture into the labyrinth of London's underground, check that the lines are working. It's not uncommon to have an entire weekend ruined by a stray leaf on the line or 'repairs to the track', which any Londoner knows stands for, 'drunken twat took a piss on the line and electrocuted his love-sack, before falling face first in front of a train. Again.'

If you do manage to make it onto a functioning tube carriage, the next stop, believe it or not, is Tooting. Yes, we know it's Zone 3, but pack your passport and get ready for a good stuffing. Tooting is renowned for its excellent curries. Take your pick of the cute restaurants in this area, but in our opinion you won't find a better one than Kastoori, a vegetarian affair that serves some freaky grub worth travelling for. Ever wanted a green banana curry? Neither had

we until we tried it. And everything here is so cheap you'll almost feel guilty for walking away so satisfied. For bargainous eats you could also head to Abbey Mills, opposite the Sainsbury's Savacentre. Here you'll find everything from fat king prawns to spicy Indonesian beef rendang, all at just three or four quid per dish.

We love a good comedy night, and there are plenty of laughs to be had at the Bedford in Balham. Voted the best pub in London twice, this is three floors of tourist-free funkiness, and some of the best comedians have performed here, including Harry Hill, Paul Tomkinson and Will Smith. It's £15 for the Banana Cabaret on Fridays and Saturdays, but it's worth every penny when you can dance 'til 2am to the Monkeyfunk DJs.

If that's your Saturday, you can fend off the hangover on Sunday with some serious lounging. The Smoke Rooms in Clapham are a firm fave for free Sunday papers, roast dinners you'll struggle to finish and squishy sofas. Or there's the Frog and Forget-Me-Not for picking up a spaced-out Aussie and a good pad Thai.

There you go: all you need do to explore the less-seen parts of London is to stock up on pre-pay or a zones 1–3 travel pass, and as long as the tubes are on your side, the world's your Oyster card.

Allo daahlin'

IT AIN'T THAT EASY TO FIND COCKNEYS IN LONDON. ASK YOUR AVERAGE CITY DWELLER THE WAY TO THE APPLES AND PEARS AND THEY'LL DIRECT YOU TO A LEBANESE GROCER'S. LUCKY FOR YOU, ITCHY KNOWS WHERE TO GO

Greasy spoons are a great place to find guvs and luvs tucking into fried bread and black pud with extra Tommy K. One of Itchy's fave spots is Islington's Alpino (97 Chapel Market, N1, 020 7837 8330), scene of Air Max-sporting, potty-mouthed prom queen Lily Allen's *Smile* video. If you need something stronger than a cuppa, and want to get legless with the Cocker-knees, go out on a limb with the old boys at The Steam Engine (41–42 Cosser Street, SE1, 020 7207 2757). Folks there may've known each other for yonks, but give 'em an hour, and they'll have your life story out of you, too.

If that makes you want to scarper, hail a black cab and utter the magic words, 'things ain't what they used to be around here,' to glean some tips on those preserved Lahndan havens that haven't yet gone to the dogs. Then go to the dogs. Don your sheepskin jacket, spark up a roll-up and go hound the punters at Walthamstow Stadium (E4, 020 8498 3300), where Becks worked in the bar as a young whippersnapper. Have yourself a little flutter from 6.30pm, every Tuesday, Thursday and Saturday.

To meet traders closer to Trotter than a little piggy's little piggies, choose somewhere more spit than polish. Skip Shoreditch and head to Billingsgate Fish Market (Trafalgar Way, Isle of Dogs, E14, Tue–Sat, 5am–8.30am) or Leather Lane Market (EC1, Mon–Fri, 10am–3pm) for hawkers and squawkers with rhyming slang sales pitches. Finally, put your own fingers in pies at M Manze, LDN's oldest pie and mash shop (87 Tower Bridge Road, SE1, 020 7407 2985), and get some grub with the best of the rest from dahn Saarf. Lovely jubbly.

Central

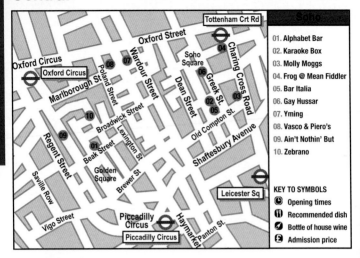

Soho

01. Alphabet Bar
02. Karaoke Box
03. Molly Moggs
04. Frog @ Mean Fiddler
05. Bar Italia
06. Gay Hussar
07. Yming
08. Vasco & Piero's
09. Ain't Nothin' But
10. Zebrano

KEY TO SYMBOLS

🕐 Opening times
🍴 Recommended dish
🍷 Bottle of house wine
🎫 Admission price

SOHO BARS

Alphabet Bar

61–63 Beak Street, W1
(020) 7439 2190
⊖ Oxford Circus

We love the downstairs area in this lively Soho hipster hangout, with its comfy sofas and huge map of London on the floor. You could sit for hours sipping the perfectly blended mojitos if you could afford to. Friday night can be a bit of a bummer, so it's best to steer clear if you don't fancy standing with your head in a media dahling's armpit (or having one in your own, if you're a tall 'un), but the crowd is fit enough to stick around for – play your cards right and you might just pull.

🕐 Mon–Fri, 12am–11pm; Sat, 4pm–11pm

Amber Bar

6 Poland Street, W1
(020) 7734 3094
⊖ Tottenham Court Road

Southern American (or Creole) cooking at its finest takes over the top part of this bustling restaurant/bar on Poland Street, while downstairs the good people of Soho dance and snog in the leather alcoves well into the night. A great place for parties this one – start early with half price bottles of wine and 2-for-1 cocktails from 5pm on weekdays. With so much cut-price sauce to pour down yourself, it's probably a good idea to line your stomach with some tapas or the chunky chips with garlic mayo. See, Itchy does encourage responsible drinking.

🕐 Mon–Fri, 12pm–1am; Sat, 5pm–1am

Bar Chocolate

26–27 D'Arblay Street, W1
(020) 7287 2823
⊖ **Oxford Circus**

It's pokier and smokier than Patsy's living room after a Friday night sesh, but they flock in droves to this teeny chocolate bar-sized eatery, purely because... well, because everyone else does. It's the place to swill down a glass of rouge with a mate, while discussing the ways of the world; it's the place to take your ex for nachos if you want somewhere they'll look bad if they turn on the whinge factor; and it's the place you can dump them all over again when you've finished licking up the last of the sour cream. Too cool for school, but we love it.

🕒 *Mon–Sat; 10am–11pm;*
Sun, 10am–10.30pm

Crobar

17 Manette Street, W1
(020) 7439 0831
⊖ **Tottenham Court Road**

Harder than masonry nails and louder than Jade Goody singing *Ace Of Spades* through a megaphone, the Crobar is heavy metal paradise if you like your music with rocks in. It's pretty small but that just means you can hear the brilliant jukebox even better and the walk to the bar is more manageable. If you think Slayer, Iron Maiden and Led Zeppelin were contestants in the last series of Robot Wars, then you're probably best giving the Crobar a wide berth. It's not exactly the place for a quiet drink...

🕒 *Mon–Sat, 1pm–3am;*
happy hour, Mon–Sat, 1pm–9pm

Ain't Nothin' But

20 Kingly Street, W1
(020) 7287 0514
⊖ **Oxford Circus**

Christ on a trike, this place is the danglies. It does exactly what it says on the tin, but without the tackiness you might expect from a theme bar. The live blues band is always exceptional and the extended sets are good enough to turn even the squarest audience into a deliriously happy, sociable mess. It does get busy, but you won't notice after five minutes. Arrive early to get in for free and avoid queues to make your eyes water.

🕒 *Mon–Wed, 6pm–1am; Thu, 6pm–2am; Fri, 6pm–3am; Sat, 2pm–3am; Sun, 3pm–12am*
🎟 *Mon–Wed & Sun, free; Thu, free before 9.30pm; Fri–Sat, free before 8.30pm; prices vary according to event at other times*

Central

Garlic & Shots

14 Frith Street, W1
(020) 7734 9505
⊖ Tottenham Court Road

Enough garlic in everything to render you not only vampire free, but friendship free too. In fact, Itchy stayed here a little too long and exited the building smelling so much like a pound of stuffed beef that we practically had the homeless following us like rats to the pied piper. It's a stinky affair, but at least consider the good all that garlic's doing to your heart as you napalm your braincells with the shots. The downstairs bar is a bastion of gothdom, so if you don't like your dancing partners lily-faced don't brush your teeth before heading down.

☺ *Mon–Wed, 5pm–12.30am; Thu–Sat, 6pm–1am; Sun, 5pm–11.30pm*

Karaoke Box Dai Chan

18 Frith Street, W1
(020) 7494 3878
⊖ Tottenham Court Road

Not quite a bar, more of an experience, but you can't live in London and not be dragged into this Frith Street fave at some point. This private karaoke establishment has several grotty rooms, the largest holding up to 12 people, and despite mics that issue nastier feedback than Simon Cowell with a migraine, it's not a cheap place to blast your lungs out. But still, where else can you belt out *I Will Survive* before falling on your face, quite clearly having survived nothing at all? Oh that's right, Lucky Voice, a much classier affair… almost.

☺ *Open daily until 1am*
✆ *From £25 per hour*

Fried and tested

If you're anything like the skinny-jean Camden brigade then breakfast is often the first and last meal of the day, so best make the most of it. **Bar Gansa** (Inverness Street, NW1, 020 7267 8909) provides a hearty fusion of Spanish cuisine and English early-morning grease, but if a healthy start to the day is a priority then the **Blue Mountain Café** (18 North Cross Road, SE22, 020 8299 6953) in East Dulwich is just the ticket. We recommend any one of their amazing smoothies. The Ferrari of fry-ups is available for the princely sum of £16.50 at **1 Lombard Street**. (1 Lombard Street, EC3, 020 7929 6611) £16.50? Are the sausages stuffed with larks' tongues and seasoned with spices grown on the north face of Everest? No, but we doubt you'd eat them if they were.

Milroy's Basement

3 Greek Street, W1

(020) 7437 2385

⊖ Tottenham Court Road

Over 700 whiskeys on offer and just never enough hours in an evening. Squirreled away beneath an off-licence of the same name, Milroy's is a teeny tiny bar devoted only to the good stuff. It's the kind of place your granddaddy would be proud to drag you down to and introduce you to the folk that kept him going in the war years, when they used to dilute the booze with fuel from the Spitfires to make it go further. If it had been open then. Sample eye-watering nectar at the bar, then stagger back upstairs for some more Greek Street treats, or just go for that kebab you'll be craving.

🕑 *Times vary*

Zebrano

14–16 Ganton Street, W1

(020) 7287 5267

⊖ Oxford Circus

This neat Soho bar is a rare beast as just about everything it does, it does well – drinks, food, décor and location are all top notch, but the real bonus is that Zebrano serves one of the finest steaks you'll ever sink your teeth into. It's the perfect place for early evening cocktails, and the popular group platters are great for snacking on as the bar begins to liven up around you. Itchy also approves of the availability of mini drinks lockers here; you can buy a bottle of something clear and strong and keep what you don't drink until your next visit.

🕑 *Mon–Wed, 11am–12am; Thu–Sat, 11am–1am; Sun, 11am–2am*

Two Floors

3 Kingly Street, W1

(020) 7439 1007

⊖ Oxford Circus

Nestled at the end of Kingly Street and without the standard flashing neon sign advertising its existence, this dimly-lit, feel-good bar is reminiscent of the one in *Cheers*, where everybody knows your name, as long as your trousers are tight enough. A bit of a media hangout, it used to be a secret, but even now that everyone knows about its funky youth club-esque interior and Mexican-style tikki lounge, it's still a pretty nice place to get to know your date. Buy them a beer upstairs, then snuggle up close later in the darkness downstairs.

🕑 *Mon–Thu, 12pm–11.30pm; Fri–Sat, 12pm–12am*

Central

SOHO PUBS

The Crown and Two Chairmen

31 Dean Street, W1

(020) 7437 8192

⊖ Tottenham Court Road

Downstairs is a very dark old pub filled with trendy people, other trendy people, and more trendy people. Battle your way upstairs and you'll be rewarded with more people in rather more incongruous setting that we reckon is more akin to 60s Waikiki. The Crown offers an upmarket selection of booze and nibbles, including syrupy cherry beers and wasabi peas, alongside the more traditional pints of wife beater and bowls of nuts.

🕒 *Mon–Sun, 11am–11pm*

The Midas Touch

4 Golden Square, W1

(020) 7287 9247

⊖ Piccadilly Circus

Some might say it's a touristy dive that reeks of stale beer and teems with indecisive travellers blocking the way to the toilets with their monstrous rucksacks. Well, we suppose they'd be right, but that's not to say this grotty pub won't charm your pants off once you've been here a while. Itchy stuck around twenty minutes waiting for a mate and by the end of that time had made three new friends over quite a decent pint. Sometimes it's not about the place, but rather the people who share it. Aaaah, how lovely.

🕒 *Mon–Sat, 12am–12pm;*
Sun, 12pm–11.30pm

The John Snow

39 Broadwick Street, W1

(020) 7437 1344

⊖ Oxford Circus

We like the big 'ol John Snow, partly because it's one of those preposterously cheap Sam Smith pubs (two quid a pint makes Itchy happy), but also because the crowd of Soho after-workers are a diverse old bunch. Incidentally, Itchy did a bit of research on this John Snow bloke. He was a renowned physician, and ironically a teetotaller. Think about that next time you're round here necking your tenth pint of cheap cider. Ideal for a thrifty and easy livener or two before heading into Soho proper.

🕒 *Mon–Fri, 12pm–11pm; Sun, 12pm–*
10.30pm; Food, Mon–Thu 12pm–2pm &
5pm–9pm; Fri, 12pm–2pm; Sat, 12pm–5pm

Molly Moggs

2 Old Compton Street, W1

(020) 7434 4294

⊖ Tottenham Court Road

A Sunday afternoon at Molly's feels like coming home after an arduous adventure. Yes it might be cramped, but the beauty of old school English pubs is in their cosiness, and you can't beat snuggling up here with a group of mates when it's pissing it down outside, if you can find some room. The décor's a bit odd though. We haven't yet worked out what's with the busts holding up the ceiling, and to be honest the glitter balls aren't really necessary when we know it's a semi-gay bar anyway. Still, Molly's might be small, but it's definitely perfectly formed.

⊙ *Mon–Sat, 11am–11pm; Sun, 6pm–10pm*

The Royal George

Goslett Yard, 133 Charing Cross Road, WC2

(020) 7734 8837

⊖ Tottenham Court Road

Tucked away down an alleyway off Charing Cross Road, you're unlikely to stumble across the Royal George unless you've drunkenly lost your way. But that's just as we like it because where the tourists can't find the pub, the locals can find a seat. Looks odd on the outside, with palm fronds and a big blue statue, but inside it has a spacious ground floor and a basement bar tucked away. Serves the usual burgers, wedges and the like, and if you're partial to nuts, this place should be your Mecca.

⊙ *Tue–Wed, 12pm–11pm;*
Thu–Sat, 12pm–1am

⑪ *Burger, £6.90*

O'Neill's

37–38 Great Malborough Street, W1

(020) 7437 0039

⊖ Oxford Circus

This pub is so Oirish it should have Ronan Keating busking outside and The Pogues as barmen, serving a potato-only menu. OK, so it's not terribly Irish, but it is a good place to socialise in W1 without venturing into some of the more pretentious bars nearby. Perfect for a pint with mates, and by the time you read this, with any luck, Westlife's career will have disastrously fallen apart and it will be them pouring your pints at the bar or bringing your chips over. Bet they can't do the little clover shape in the froth though; that takes talent.

⊙ *Mon–Thu, 10am–11pm;*
Fri, 10am–11.30pm; Sun, 10am–11pm

The Toucan

19 Carlisle Street, W1

(020) 7437 4123

⊖ Tottenham Court Road

A tiny little pub situated just off the very pleasant Soho Square, The Toucan specialises in serving the finest Guinness and Irish whiskey to a discerning crowd. They also serve decent traditional-style sandwiches in the basement bar and have regular entertainment, should the thought of splashing out £40 on one measure of single malt not be comedy enough. Fortunately, they do some cheaper whiskies as well so if you're a fan of the hard stuff then the 30 or so varieties on offer will send you careering ecstatically into the middle of next week.

⊙ *Mon–Sat, 11am–11pm*

Central

SOHO CLUBS

Frog @ the Mean Fiddler

165 Charing Cross Road, WC2
(020) 7434 9592
⊖ Tottenham Court Road

If you give a monkey's about your music then this is your club. They have at least one live band playing every week and the atmosphere is legendary – sticky floors, pints in plastic glasses and the Converse and greasy hair brigade, whose crazy moves make for half the fun. The other half of the enjoyment is provided by excellent DJs playing a wide mix of indie tunes over two separate rooms.
☻ *Opening times vary according to event*
☻ *£5 with flyer before 12am, £7 with flyer after 12am, £10 without flyer*

Strawberry Moons

15 Heddon Street, W1
(020) 7437 7300
⊖ Oxford Circus

This is what Itchy likes to call a 'Marmite club'. Sorry? Err, no, that's not exactly what we meant. What we're saying is you'll either love it or hate it here. It's a big, throbbing mix of confused chavs, lonely foreign businessmen and flirty pretty boys, all getting down to the filthiest tunes ever to come out of the big pop machine. If you like your music so cheesy you can still smell it on your clothes the next day, then this is your night.
☻ *Mon, 5pm–12am; Tue–Wed, 5pm–2am; Thu–Sat, 5pm–3am*
☻ *Mon–Wed, free; Thu, £5 after 10pm; Fri, 9pm–10pm, £5; 10pm–close, £7; Sat, 8pm–9pm, £5; 9pm–10pm, £8; 10pm–close, £10*

Heavy Load @ The Phoenix

37 Cavendish Square, W1
(020) 7493 8003
⊖ Oxford Circus

Back in the 60s, psychedelica was born just up the road in Soho, and it lives on at Heavy Load, the monthly 60s and 70s rock night held at The Phoenix pub. Walk down the steps to the pub's basement and you'll be stepping back to a time when you'd have been wearing flowery shirts, hippy dresses and leather waistcoats. The atmosphere's incredibly friendly, and almost as much fun as blasting back to 1966, putting a bet on England winning the footy and spending your winnings on a summer of free loving and festivals.
☻ *Last Sat of the month, 10pm–late*
☻ *£5*

The Tatty Bogle Club

11 Kingly Court, Kingly Street, W1
(020) 7734 4475
⊖ Oxford Circus

Recently re-opened after six months of renovations, this Soho dancing spot is now bigger and better than ever before, with live music Mondays to Thursdays, and DJs at the weekends. It used to be a fave with The Beatles back in the day, but we don't reckon the Evostick floors, beer-drenched tables and slurring luvvies this place has been attracting for a while would have been their cup of tea. Still, let's hope they don't change it too much. It wouldn't be the same if the smell of paint overpowered that of piss at weekends. Members only, but entry is totally blaggable, believe us.
☻ *Mon–Sat, 9pm–3.30am*

SOHO CAFÉS

Amato

14 Old Compton Street, W1

(020) 734 5733

⊖ Leicester Square

Any place with Marilyn Monroe beckoning you inside to a calorie-laden spread has to be a winner in our books. Once you're done pawing the windows and drooling over the cakes, take a seat in a dark wooden chair and finger the comforting maroon table tops. Sniff the smell of fresh roasted coffee that fills the place, and relish the sight of Soho divas scoffing croissants at the speed of light before someone reminds them they're supposed to be a size zero.

☻ *Mon–Sat, 8am–10pm; Sun, 10am–8pm*

❿ *Mixed berry tart, £3.25*

Café at Foyles

113–119 Charing Cross Road, WC2

(020) 7440 3207

⊖ Tottenham Court Road

Itchy has never had such an excellent chorizo toasted sarnie, and at less than three quid it's bang on the money. This new top-floor café shares its space with Ray's Jazz, though you won't find much to jazz you off, except perhaps the service. Heeellloooo, there's only five people in here, why does it take half an hour to make eye contact? We love the chocolate brownies though, just like mum used to make but without the guilt trip. Plus the warming soups are wondrous.

☻ *Mon–Sat, 8.30am–9pm;*
Sun, 9am–6.30pm

❿ *Fennel, salami and rocket sarnie, £4*

Bar Italia

22 Frith Street, W1

(020) 7437 4520

⊖ Tottenham Court Road

A total London institution in the heart of Soho, there's no better place to wolf a cake at 5am and chat nonsense to the tripped out clubbers who aren't quite sure where they are, or why the music's stopped. Itchy loves the muddled atmosphere of strung up sausages, frothy mugs of mocha and an oversized poster of boxer Rocky Marciano by the fruit machine. In the mornings it's a fave for cabbies, but there's always a random passed out on one of the red leather stools.

☻ *Open 24 hours a day, 7 days a week*

❿ *Cheese, parma ham and*
tomato sandwich, £5.50

Central

Café Emm

17 Frith Street, W1

(020) 7437 0723

⊖ Tottenham Court Road

You can hear the clamour of this place a mile off. Simple food at excellent prices keeps 'em coming, and it's so noisy at times it's a wonder they don't issue earplugs. It's a British affair, easy on the wallet and slap bang in the middle of Soho. Fancy some Karaoke Box action after dinner? You won't even have to leave Frith Street.

⦿ *Mon–Thu, 12pm–2.30pm & 5.30pm–10.30pm; Fri, 12pm–2.30pm & 5.30pm–11.30pm; Sat, 1pm–12.30am; Sun, 1pm–10.30pm*

⓫ *Lamb shank braised with garlic and herbs, £9.95*

◕ *£10.95*

Maoz Vegetarian

43 Old Compton Street, W1

(020) 7851 1586

⊖ Leicester Square

Not the place to head for if you're looking for slick décor or romantic atmosphere, as you won't find either here. It's plain, brightly-lit, and if you manage to get a table it'll undoubtedly be littered with discarded serviettes and empty bottles. But by the time you get your mitts on the cooked-to-order falafel your only worry will be how much you can stuff into your pitta bread. There's an impressive range of fillings to stuff them with as well – sublime fried cauliflower, pickled radish, and too many chilli sauces to list.

⦿ *Sun–Thu, 11am–1am; Fri–Sat, 11am–2am*

⓫ *Falafel and hummus, £3.80*

SOHO RESTAURANTS

Alastair Little

49 Frith Street, W1

(020) 7734 5183

⊖ Tottenham Court Road

A bit off the beaten track and avoiding the tourists by a hair's breadth, this tiny Itchy fave from the talented fingers of pioneering UK chef Alastair Little himself serves modern British food in a rather stark, minimalist atmosphere that somehow still manages to be friendly and unassuming. Beware though, British food it well might be, but it's nothing you could copy in your own kitchen.

⦿ *Mon–Fri, 12pm–3pm & 6pm–11pm; Sat, 6pm–11pm*

⓫ *Lunch, £38 for three courses*

◕ *£17.50*

Aperitivo

41 Beak Street, W1

(020) 7287 2057

⊖ Piccadilly Circus/Oxford Circus

Italian tapas? It'll never take off. Sorry? It already has? Well best all head down to this Beak Street treat which promotes the concept of sharing and enjoying. So not one for the selfish or starving. Itchy headed down with a group of six and was able to share a good few dishes; the ravioli filled with cheese in a butter and sage sauce was to die for. The staff are really sweet, and not the types to rush you out when you're done, so hang about and sip rocket fuel coffee. Bellissimo.

⊕ *Mon–Sat, 12pm–11pm*

⊕ *Grilled lamb cutlets, £6.50*

⊘ *£13.50*

Bar Shu

28 Frith Street, W1

(020) 7287 6688

⊖ Leicester Square

Recruiting five chefs from the same region isn't usually difficult for a restaurant, but when they're all from Sichuan it's a different story. This new restaurant puts most of its surrounding Chinatown to shame with its stylish three–storey sex appeal and Yauatcha–blue lighting. We love the Sichuan opera masks beaming out at us while we eat. You might want to steer clear of the 'man and wife offal slices' – ox heart, tripe and tongue, apparently. Bleurgh. Watch out for the hot Eastern dishes too.

⊕ *Mon–Sun, 12pm–12am*

⊕ *Sea bass in extremely spicy soup, £28*

⊘ *£14.50*

Bam-Bou

1 Percy Street, W1

(020) 7323 9130

⊖ Goodge Street

Itchy always likes a bit of glamour in its life, and the cocktails here make us feel oh-so special (even at £7 a pop), while the Vietnamese cooking is enough to lure in punters looking for posh nosh – the peppered beef dish will melt in your mouth and leave you seriously considering ordering the same again. The portions are quite stingy for the price, but ain't that always how you can tell it's good?

⊕ *Mon–Fri, 12pm–3pm & 6pm–11.30pm; Sat, 6pm–11.30pm*

⊕ *Peppered beef fillet with kow choi and shaoshing, £12.50*

⊘ *£15*

Gay Hussar

2 Greek Street, W1

(020) 7437 0973

⊖ Tottenham Court Road

Think of the great cuisines and Hungarian probably ranks just slightly above war rations. However, the Gay Hussar offers authentic Hungarian fare that is both hearty and tasty. The surroundings, with walls adorned with books aplenty and caricatures of politicians make for a very comfortable dining experience, and it feels like you might be a guest of honour in someone's home.

⊕ *Mon–Sat, 12.15pm–2.30pm & 5.30pm–10.45pm*

⊕ *Kolozsvári töltött káposzta (stuffed cabbage, sauerkraut, smoked bacon and sausage), £12.50*

⊘ *£13.95*

Central

Hummus Bros

88 Wardour Street, W1

(020) 7734 1311

⊖ Tottenham Court Road/Oxford Circus

So, who did put the 'mmmm' in hummus? The answer is, of course, the Hummus Brothers, who've been dishing up their own special recipe since their hard-up student days, when they hardly had two chickpeas to rub together. Now providing hummus to the impoverished masses, the selfless Bros also donate any leftovers to charity. Healthy and virtuous lunches on a shoestring – what more could you possibly want?

Ⓒ *Mon–Wed, 11am–10pm; Thu–Fri, 11am–11pm; Sat, 12pm–11pm*

Ⓘ *Hummus (astonishingly) with chunky beef stew topping, £5*

Ⓓ *Not licensed*

The Stockpot

18 Old Compton Street, W1

(020) 7287 1066

⊖ Leicester Square

If The Stockpot were a car it would be a Morris Minor: robust, reliable and reassuringly old-fashioned. Something of a London institution, this small Soho eatery has been serving up steaming plates of nourishing, canteen-style grub for years. Ok, it will never win accolades for haute cuisine. But where else can you fill your belly with prawn cocktail, followed by beef stroganoff, plus treacle sponge and custard, and all for around a tenner?

Ⓒ *Mon–Sat, 11.30am–12am; Sun, 11.30am–11.30pm*

Ⓘ *Fried liver, £3.95*

Ⓓ *£8.60*

Pure California

39 Beak Street, W1

(020) 7287 3708

⊖ Piccadilly Circus

Healthy fast food? No, you're not dreaming, you're just experiencing another case of American denial. Still, we suppose a menu of soups, smoothies and salads does sort of override the other less nutritious US fare in the vicinity. The sweet Thai chicken wrap comes in at just under three quid and with sides like potato salad starting at £1.95, there are more expensive places to get fit on the inside. A tasty welcome treat to Soho; now all you need is the boob job.

Ⓒ *Mon–Thu, 7.30am–7.30pm; Fri, 7.30am–6pm; Sat, 11am–6pm; Sun, 11am–6pm*

Ⓘ *Prawn and avocado wrap, £2.95*

Ⓓ *Small smoothie, £2.65*

Thai Cottage

34 D'Arblay Street, W1

(020) 7439 7099

⊖ Oxford Circus

It might look like a grotty noodle bar in the middle of tourist-land, but we think you'll find the food in this little Thai trinket is pretty authentic. Itchy loves the no-frills atmosphere at Cottage – what you see is what you get. The shrimp starter with spicy sauce is delicious, not too salty and not so filling that you won't be ready for a scrummy main of fried chicken. Don't go to the loo though, you'll be in for a shock.

Ⓒ *Mon–Thu, 12pm–4pm & 5.30pm–10.30pm; Fri, 12pm–4pm & 5.30pm–11pm; Sat, 5.30pm–11pm*

Ⓘ *Green curry, £6.75*

Ⓓ *£8.95*

Vasco and Piero's Pavilion

15 Poland Street, W1

(020) 7437 8774

⊖ Oxford Circus

This little Italian has become something of a hidden treasure for many of its regular customers, including the king of theatreland himself, Sir Andrew Lloyd Webber, who rocked up half way through our tortelloni. It's classy enough to feel special, but not in a pretentious way, and the food is melt-in-the-mouth tasty, especially the fresh filled pasta. Not so good for the mushroom-phobic though.

🕒 *Mon–Fri, 12pm–2.30pm & 6pm–10.45pm; Sat, 6pm–10.45pm*

🍴 *Handmade wild mushroom tortelloni with girolles, £12.50*

💷 *£12.50*

Yming

35–36 Greek Street, W1

(020) 7734 2721

⊖ Leicester Square

Personally, we're 'Itching' to go back to Yming for some more excellent North Chinese grub. Frequented by a lot of PR yuppies so you may not get a table at peak times, this place has an intimate atmosphere, excellent food and service, and is reasonably priced as far as central London goes. The service is attentive and they are always happy to adapt dishes to personal taste. Heaven or what? Well, as with the real thing, only if you can get past the door.

🕒 *Mon–Sat, 12pm–11.45pm*

🍴 *Fixed lunch menu, £15*

💷 *£16*

VitaOrganic

74 Wardour Street, W1

(020) 7734 8986

⊖ Tottenham Court Road/Oxford Circus

If munching through a bloody steak is your idea of misery, you'd do much better ploughing through a ploughman's at this organic, veggie and vegan restaurant. Cooking with the firm belief that pure food equals a pure mind in an age of toxins, you won't find anything microwaved or deep fat fried in this place. With dishes like cauliflower and celery salad and purple onion cabbage soup, you might be farting like a donkey for a week, but at least your innards will be glowing.

🕒 *Mon–Sat, 12pm–10pm; Sun, 12pm–9pm*

🍴 *Orange sweet potato dhal, £3.90*

🥤 *Green rejuvenator juice, £3.90*

Central

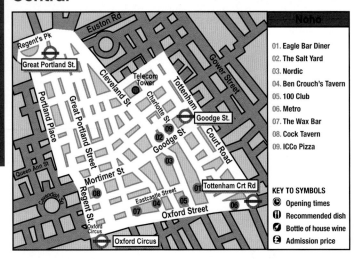

Noho

01. Eagle Bar Diner
02. The Salt Yard
03. Nordic
04. Ben Crouch's Tavern
05. 100 Club
06. Metro
07. The Wax Bar
08. Cock Tavern
09. ICCo Pizza

KEY TO SYMBOLS

🕐 Opening times

🍴 Recommended dish

🍷 Bottle of house wine

💷 Admission price

NOHO BARS

Eagle Bar Diner

3–5 Rathbone Place, W1

(020) 7637 1418

⊖ Tottenham Court Road/Goodge Street

Trendy bar and burger house that doesn't serve birds of prey, but does do a nice line in beef-based fodder. And an emu burger, which is kind of like an eagle. The burgers are some of the finest you'll ever encounter, while their chocolate malts are worth killing for, although you may rupture yourself trying to get it through the straw.

🕐 *Mon–Wed, 12pm–11pm; Thu–Fri, 12pm–1am; Sat, 10am–1am; Sun, 11am–6pm*

🍴 *6oz Mexican burger, £6.95*

🍷 *Peanut butter and banana malt shake, £3.75*

Firevault

36 Great Titchfield Street, W1

(020) 7636 2091

⊖ Oxford Circus

What better way to warm the cockles of your heart than having a cocktail or two in a working fireplace showroom? The interior's cool white and minimalist, rather than the log fire-heated cabin you'd expect, but it's still a cosy way to pass an hour or two, particularly if it's a bit nippy outside. Cocktails range from the classics (shaken not stirred) to scary-sounding 'round the world trip' packages with seven cocktails from countries across the globe. Get stuck into the group-friendly bar menu to soak up some booze.

🕐 *Mon–Fri, 12pm–11pm; Sat, 6pm–11pm; Food from 6pm*

🍷 *Cocktails, from £8*

Jerusalem

33–34 Rathbone Place, W1

(020) 7255 1120

⊖ Tottenham Court Road/Goodge Street

It's a fair size, classy, known for some half-decent food and can be fairly busy in the evenings. No, we're not talking about Michael 'but I'm a good driver' Winner but a very nice basement bar in Fitzrovia which comes well recommended, whether for those en-masse evening gatherings or just a quiet lunchtime visit. The décor is interesting (in a good way on this occasion) but the drinks are a little bit dear compared to some of the nearby pubs.

Ⓒ Mon, 12pm–11pm; Tue–Wed, 12pm–12am; Thu–Fri, 12pm–1am; Sat, 7pm–1am

Ⓜ Mon–Thu, two courses for £10

Ⓐ £14.50

Nordic

25 Newman Street, W1

(020) 7631 3174

⊖ Goodge Street/Tottenham Court Road

Like the A-Team, this bar is great if you can find it. It's more Face than BA, seeing as it's quite small in comparison to its peers, but almost perfectly formed (it's also quite hot of an evening). An adaptable bar, Nordic is a good place to go for a few quick and quiet daytime drinks or a mental weekend vodka binge. After all, vodka, so we hear, is your average Scandinavian's water substitute, so have a taste of some of the numerous varieties on offer and soak the booze up with some excellent Nordic–style snacks. Skol.

Ⓒ Mon–Fri, 11.30am–11.30pm; Sat, 5pm–12am; Sun, 12pm–12.30am

Long Bar

Sanderson Hotel, 50 Berners Street, W1

(020) 7851 6969

⊖ Goodge Street

Did you ever see that old film, *The Explorers* with River Phoenix and Ethan Hawke? When the alien kid gives them a little round thing and tells him it's 'the stuff that dreams are made of'? Well they were wrong. The stuff that dreams are made of is the 80-foot bar in this place. It's the joint to come and sit while you're waiting for someone rich to spot your potential as a trophy wife/hubby. The sexy bar staff pour cocktails to die for while the clientele flash jewels the size of houses. It's never gonna be your local, but this hotel bar is escapism you won't forget in a hurry.

Ⓒ Mon–Sat, 10am–1am; Sun, 10am–11pm

The Salt Yard

54 Goodge Street, W1

(020) 7637 0657

⊖ Goodge Street

In need of a cosy yet achingly hip venue for that make or break date? Fear ye not, readers. Walk in and you'll find chic chocolate decor with an intimate layout to ensure you make your sweet nothings heard. Table service means you can be wooing rather than queuing, while secretly ordering dishes like the Calasparra rice pudding brulée with rhubarb ice cream while your intended is in the loo will certainly seal the deal.

Ⓒ Mon–Fri, 12pm–11pm; Sat, 5pm–11pm

Ⓜ Calasparra rice pudding brulée with rhubarb ice cream, £4.50

Ⓐ £3.50 a glass

Central

NOHO PUBS

Ben Crouch's Tavern

77a Wells Street, W1
(020) 7636 0717
⊖ Oxford Circus

Like a secret portal to special Harry Potter drinking world, the Crouch nestles on an Oxford Circus back street, invisible to the eyes of muggles. Or at least it feels that way with its wrought iron entrance, gargoyle strewn innards, cackling toilets and 'seven deadly sins' cocktail test tubes. Drinks offers mean that it needn't be an expensive night, but get there early to claim one of the hideaway holes in its winding interior. If only they served Butterbeer...

© *Mon–Sat, 11am–11pm;*
Sun, 12pm–10.30pm

Cock Tavern

27 Great Portland Street, W1
(020) 7631 5002
⊖ Oxford Circus

Dreary, tacky-carpeted and crowded? Or wonderfully ornate and old-fashioned? Whichever description you think fits best, you'll have to admit that the Cock is a true honest-to-God pub, nestled amongst the trendier bars of Fitzrovia. Samuel Smith beverage lovers, West End workers and bods from the Beeb pack out the bijou ground and first floor bars – spilling onto the street in summer – all the while delighting in the bloody-cheap-for-London prices.

© *Mon–Sat, 11.30am–11pm; Sun, 12pm–10.30pm; Food, Mon–Thu 12pm–2.30pm & 6pm–8.30pm; Fri, 12pm–2.30pm; Sat–Sun, 12pm–6pm*

NOHO CLUBS

The 100 Club

100 Oxford Street, W1

(020) 7636 0933

⊖ Tottenham Court Road/Oxford Circus

This place is truly legendary – half your CD collection will have probably played there and as for the other half, well you shouldn't be buying stuff by Daniel O'Donnell anyway so we'll forget it. Situated right on the busier-than-Darren-Day's-bedroom end of Oxford Street, it may not look much but once inside you'll soon warm to its slightly dated décor. The 100 Club also hosts regular club nights featuring a wide range of excellent music.

ⓒ *Times and prices vary according to event*

Metro

19–23 Oxford Street, W1

(020) 7636 7744

⊖ Tottenham Court Road

One of Itchy's favourite Friday night haunts. You just can't beat having a cold can in your hand while dancing away to some classic indie cuts, surrounded by a great mix of people. It's great fun and they also feature regular gigs during the week and on Friday evenings before the club night starts. So if you've ever wandered down Oxford Street at 11.30pm and wondered what the queue is just along from Tottenham Court Road tube, then wonder no longer. Blowup, held every Friday night after the gig, is well worth a look.

ⓒ *Times and prices vary according to event*

Astoria

157 Charing Cross Road, WC2

(020) 7434 9592

⊖ Tottenham Court Road

It's so close to the tube that you could launch that wannabe goth in the queue right back down into the subway (with the help of a lucky deflection) and take their place before anybody notices. And this might be a good idea as you'd be more likely to slide in there and see one of the many excellent bands who play the Astoria, or get into their legendary GAY night, if that's your scene. Check out the listings well in advance as most gigs and nights sell out weeks and months before you'd otherwise think about it.

ⓒ *Times and prices vary according to event*

Central

The Roxy

3 Rathbone Place, W1

(020) 7255 1098

⊖ Tottenham Court Road/Goodge Street

If your mates have a collective musical taste as diverse as a Tory MP's selection of mistresses then you're on to a winner. Just lure them off Oxford Street and as the inevitable debate about where to go next unfolds, propose the Roxy. As they quiver with fear reassure them with 'They'll probably play stuff like Abba, Blur, Libertines, Stone Roses some Village People and maybe a bit of Madonna if you ask', at which point they'll dash for the entrance and proceed to have a really good night.

🄯 *Mon–Thu, 5pm–3am; Fri, 5pm–3.30am; Sat, 9.30pm–3.30am*

🄴 *Mon–Thu, £5; Fri–Sat, £4–£9*

NOHO CAFÉS

Bar Remo

2 Princes Street, W1

(020) 7629 1715

⊖ Oxford Circus

Do not go here. Why? The huge portions of good value, Italian dishes, the welcoming staff, the overwhelming sarnies (all served with crisps), the walls lined with wine bottles and faded photos of faded celebrities. Go to Pret, Eat, M&S, anywhere, but stay away from this wondrous little place. It's all ours. We're still unable to finish the San Moritz – the most filling, most delicious, artery-hardening mixture of spinach, cheese and bacon on focaccia. Oh dear, we've eaten too much again.

🄯 *Mon–Sat, 8.30am–5pm*

The Wax Bar

4 Winsley Street, W1

(020) 7436 4650

⊖ Oxford Circus

Itchy always likes clubs with a staircase at the front – it makes us feel elite and underground – and as a post-work bevvie stop, the Wax ticks all the right boxes with its mix of cocktails, funky tunes and the suited and booted of Oxford Street. If you clock off early enough to catch happy hour from 5pm–7pm you'll find half price cocktails and bar grub. We particularly recommend the mojitos, which boast enough greenery to fulfil your five-a-day in one happy glug.

🄯 *Mon–Sat, 12pm–3am*

🄴 *Mon–Thu, free; Fri, £7 after 10pm; Sat, £10 after 9pm*

🄳 *£11.95*

Café @ Sotheby's

34–35 New Bond Street, W1

(020) 7293 5077

⊖ Bond Street

So you've spent the last two hours trudging up and down Bond Street in an effort to out-shop even Mrs Beckham. You're a little peckish, and you can barely lift all the Tiffany and Ralph Lauren bags, (or at least the chauffeur's looking a little knackered). Fanciful perhaps, but there are few better places for refreshment than the Café in the grand hall of Sotheby's. It's terribly civilised, with a great selection of sandwiches and other lunch-y fare, so if you're not coincidentally there to bid for a diamond or two, drop in anyway.

🄯 *Mon–Fri, 9.30am–5pm*

🄳 *£11.50*

NOHO RESTAURANTS

ICCo Pizza

46 Goodge Street, W1
(020) 7580 9688
⊖ Goodge Street

This staple of the Noho lunch crowd laughs in a moustachioed Italian way at the soggy Dolmio and cheddar on a stale base that are the usual British violations of the art of lunchtime pizza. Here you'll find massive shareable pizzas averaging a mere £3.50, served in a whizzing, chrome clad New Yawk-esque environment. The only problem you'll face is the difficulty in achieving anything in the afternoon after gorging yourself on ICCo's finest.
🕒 *Mon–Fri, 7am–11pm; Sat, 9am–11pm*
🍴 *Margherita pizza, £3*

Ooze

62 Goodge Street, W1
(020) 7436 9444
⊖ Goodge Street

Finally, a restaurant that serves risotto on demand, and does it well. This new addition to the culinary scene brings a touch of glam to the old Italian fave. Using nothing but proper carnaroli rice cooked in a variety of stocks, it oozes simplicity as much as flavour and will have you begging Oliver Twist-style for more. Huge salads are well worth the price, as is the yummy old school dessert, baked Alaska. Mmmm. Another one to take a date to – it's busy but not intrusive. A definite new Itchy favourite.
🕒 *Mon–Sat, 12pm–11pm*
🍴 *Hazelnut and sage risotto, £7*
💰 *£12.95*

Maze

10–13 Grosvenor Square, W1
(020) 7107 0000
⊖ Bond Street

F$%*ing hell it's another c&*%ing Gordon Ramsay gaff. And what a gaff it is – this is the place to be if you're out to impress. It's everything you would want from the big man – not a kitchen nightmare in sight. Yes you'll need to forego your beer for a few weeks as dinner with wine here is going to hurt your wallet, but it's worth it. The menu's full of things you will have never heard of, but staff are among the most approachable you'll ever meet, so don't be afraid to ask.
🕒 *Mon–Sun, 12pm–2.30pm & 6pm–10.30pm; bar, Mon–Sun, 12pm–1am*
🍴 *Four course set lunch menu, £28.50*
💰 *£17*

Ping Pong

45 Great Marlborough Street, W1
(020) 7851 6969
⊖ Oxford Circus

At long last, decent dim sum any time of the day or night rather than just lunchtimes, and a funky venue with entertaining toilets into the bargain. This buzzing, fast-paced, original venue works efficiently, the food is excellent and cheap, and the chain seems to be expanding across London faster than Jamie Oliver's waistband. You can't book, so either get there early or, cunningly, get a drink at the bar and nab yourself a table number should one magically appear in your hand...
🕒 *Mon–Sat, 12pm–12am;*
Sun, 12pm–10.30pm
🍴 *Roast pork puffs, £2.99 each*
💰 *£14*

Central

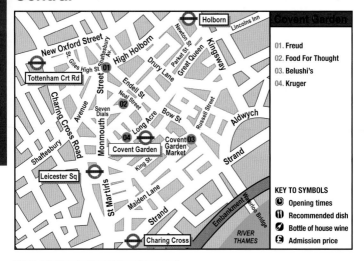

Covent Garden

01. Freud
02. Food For Thought
03. Belushi's
04. Kruger

KEY TO SYMBOLS
- 🕐 Opening times
- 🍴 Recommended dish
- 🍷 Bottle of house wine
- 🎫 Admission price

COVENT GARDEN BARS

Belushi's

9 Russell Street, WC2
(020) 7240 3411
⊖ Covent Garden

A slice of unabashed fun in the chic surroundings of Covent Garden. Indie rock royalty look down on you from the walls and the clientele range from the multi-pierced to freshly pressed 'young professionals'. Admittedly, Belushi's has a touch of the hovel bar about it – the floor has been known to stick to your shoes and when busy there's not room to swing a caterpillar, but who cares, it's loud and fun, and house wine is under a tenner.

🕐 *Mon–Sat, 11am–12am;*
Sun, 12pm–10.30pm

Freud

198 Shaftesbury Avenue, WC2
(020) 7240 9933
⊖ Tottenham Court/Covent Garden

Was Freud a fraud? That classically-worded GCSE Religious Studies question. And it would seem that the answer is 'yes'. All that time he claimed that everything was just about sex, sex, sex, and then what does he do but come to London and try and persuade us it's about booze, booze, booze? With an atmosphere like a French absinthe café and a clientele as mixed up as the drinks menu, the talented and tattooed bar staff of Freud knock up cocktails with a kick. And these babies just (Freudian) slip down a treat. The big old fraud would be proud.

🕐 *Mon–Sat, 11am–11.30pm;*
Sun, 12pm–10.30pm

COVENT GARDEN CAFÉS

Food for Thought

31 Neal Street, WC2

(020) 7836 0239

⊖ Covent Garden

A word of warning – if you're the kind of person who owns a 'Save a Cow, eat a Vegetarian' car sticker, you may find the following a little upsetting: veggie restaurant Food for Thought is a must-try, meat or no meat. Food is piled inexplicably high on your plate for less than the price of a pint at many Covent Garden pubs. Sumptuous homemade cakes and a BYO wine policy make this budget eatery near perfect.

🕒 Mon–Sat, 9.30am–8.30pm;
Sun, 12pm–5pm

🍴 Quiche with all salads, £6.30

Kruger

11 Long Acre, WC2

⊖ Leicester Square

An addition to the smoothie revolution, Kruger is a no-messing juice and smoothie bar which proffers a long list of concoctions, freshly squeezed in front of you by the efficient, fast-juicing staff. Choose from wholesome, five-a-day beverages like the 'instant energiser', yoghurt or banana based smoothies, or if you reckon your muscles can take it, opt for one containing an ultra-healthy and unpronounceable wonder-berry such as acerola or acai. And if all that sounds too healthy by far, don't despair – you can nourish your body with juice then feed your soul with cheese toasties.

🕒 Times vary

🍴 Medium juice, £2.25; large juice, £3

Central

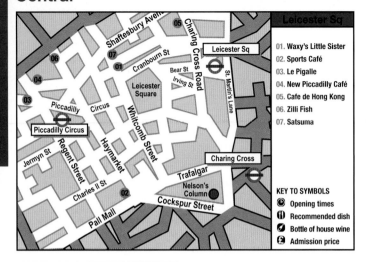

Leicester Sq

01. Waxy's Little Sister
02. Sports Café
03. Le Pigalle
04. New Piccadilly Café
05. Cafe de Hong Kong
06. Zilli Fish
07. Satsuma

KEY TO SYMBOLS

🕒 Opening times
🍴 Recommended dish
🍷 Bottle of house wine
🎟 Admission price

LEICESTER SQUARE BARS

Jewel
4–6 Glasshouse Street, W1
(020) 7439 4990
⊖ Piccadilly Circus

Visiting Jewel is a bit like going to Disneyland and finding it full of OAPs. It's the kind of place that blatantly opened in the hope of attracting London's glitterati, but actually pulls in out-of-towners dolled up and expecting to rub shoulders with Peaches Geldof. In other words, it's what you would expect from a bar slap bang in the middle of Piccadilly Circus. The champagne cocktails are worth a glug though if you do end up here.

🕒 *Mon–Thu, 5pm–1am; Fri–Sat, 4pm–1am; Sun, 6pm–12.30am*

Sports Café
80 Haymarket, SW1
(020) 7839 8300
⊖ Piccadilly Circus

Every town or district has their sports bar, a sort of Wetherspoonified drinking den with more TVs than a hooky council estate lock-up, and we are so grateful that this end of central London is no different. How pleased we are to drink lager in the shadow of an F1 car, marvel at the signed sports memorabilia and ogle the waitresses in their short skirts. Well we're not actually really pleased about most of that but it is a decent destination for any sort of popular sporting event and it can boast a brilliant atmosphere when busy.

🕒 *Mon–Sun, 12pm–3am*

🎟 *£3 before 10.30pm on weekdays; £5 at weekends*

LEICESTER SQUARE PUBS

Waxy's Little Sister

20 Wardour Street, W1
(020) 7287 8987
⊖ Leicester Square

Sister to the Irish Waxy's round the corner, this little pub covers two floors and is one of the cosiest in town. It remains relatively tourist-free upstairs, and the leather sofas prove suitable hangouts on a cold and wintry day, when Guinness, Benson and Hedges, a packet of cheese and onion crisps and an afternoon watching the amusing dumb-waiter slide up and down is all you could possibly desire. It's all about the little things.

ⓒ *Mon–Fri, 12pm–11pm; Sat, 11am–11pm; Sun, 12pm–10.30pm*

LEICESTER SQUARE CLUBS

The Burlington Club

12 New Burlington Street, W1
(020) 3102 3060
⊖ Piccadilly Circus

Proving that mere mortals like us can get a whiff of the Chanel-scented action too, this ultra-luxe club serves Basque-style tapas to hoi polloi and gods alike until 10.30pm, at which point we all turn into pumpkins and the deities party on in blissful seclusion. At least it means you can just about make last orders elsewhere.

ⓒ *Mon–Tue, 12pm–1am; Wed, 12pm–2am; Thu–Sat, 12pm–3am; Food 12pm–10:30pm*
ⓐ *Members only after 10.30pm*
(annual membership £300)
ⓞ *£16*

CC Club

13 Coventry Street, W1
(020) 7297 3200
⊖ Piccadilly Circus

One of the better late night destinations in and around Leicester Square... actually, to be honest it'll feel like a palace of heavenly wonder compared to some of the godawful dives you could end up in in this part of town. And we have. Never let it be said Itchy hasn't suffered in the pursuit of after-hours knowledge. The CC Club has some comfy seating arrangements and a number of different areas for you and your mates to make use of. If you like your music commercial but with a touch of class then you should be properly chuffed at finding this place.

ⓒ *Fri–Sat, 10pm–3am*

Central

Le Pigalle

215 Piccadilly, W1

(020) 7734 8142

⊖ Piccadilly Circus

Glamour personified, Le Pigalle is a cool 1940s supper club, all mirrors and red velvet seating, where the women are dames and the men are men (although some of them are trying to be cads, sir!). Filled with jazz bands, lone live crooners, and playing host to A-list stars such as Van the Man, this is the joint to dress up, dig out that cigarette holder as long as your arm, and vive Left Bank Paris. Dinner is served from 8pm, and is part and parcel of the whole experience.

🎸 *Mon–Wed, 7pm–2am; Thu–Sat, 7pm–3am*

🎫 *Prices vary according to event*

💷 *£16*

Tiger Tiger

29 Haymarket, SW1

(020) 7930 1885

⊖ Piccadilly Circus

Like the barmaid/man in your local that you'd probably stagger home with if your booze consumption matched their lack of looks, Tiger Tiger is best enjoyed half-cut. Otherwise the cheesy music and general emphasis on appealing to the less-discerning customer will prove annoying. On the plus side the Grill restaurant serves up some very decent Asian food as well as the old favourites and it's in a classy part of town. Many say that if you don't take a date here, you go home with one. Good luck with that, and with the strict dress code.

🎸 *Times and prices vary according to event*

Different strokes

On the first Saturday of every month head to 93 Feet East (150 Brick Lane, EC1, 020 7247 3293) for **It's Bigger Than**, a club night that aims to be 'the best house party in the history of house partying'. For the most alternative fun you can have, it's all about **Stompin'** at The 100 Club (100 Oxford Street, W1, 08713 323 707). It's a swing dance night, starting with a quick lesson at 7.45pm where you're taught the basics and a couple of routines, then you cut loose and party like it's 1949 (but without the rationing). Depression has never been so fun as at the Bar Academy Islington's **Feeling Gloomy** (16 Parkfield Street, N1, 08700 600 100) that takes place every Saturday, playing sad songs to make you happy. The highlight has to be a performance by The Miserablists, the world's best and only indie air guitar band.

LEICESTER SQUARE CAFÉS

Bar Bruno

101 Wardour Street, W1

(020) 7734 3750

⊖ Piccadilly Circus

The traditional caff seems to be a dying breed these days and as such it's getting increasingly difficult to find endless mugs of good orange tea and portions to make your heart thankful for the milk of human kindness. So all hail Bar Bruno in Soho, run by those connoisseurs of the café world, the Italians. Think myriad sandwich combos and monster fry-ups, all for mere pennies; it's manna from heaven. Looks tiny, but it's strangely vast inside.

◉ *Mon–Sat, 5am–10pm*

◐ *Egg, bacon and sausage, £3*

Gaby's Deli

30 Charing Cross Road, WC2

(020) 7836 4233

⊖ Leicester Square

Regret is a terrible thing, particularly when it comes to us after parting with hard-earned pennies for sub-standard food. This packed café-style eatery promises 'the best falafel in London' on the street-board. They say that promises are made to be broken, and this one might do just that with falafel that actually tastes a little like sawdust and hummus that isn't the best either. The service is quite dismissive, and even if you're one of those who just has to get their regular dose of chick pea, there are probably better places in the area.

◉ *Mon–Sun, 11am–12am*

◐ *Falafel sandwich and drink, £4.30*

Café de Hong Kong

47 Charing Cross Road, WC2

(020) 7534 9898

⊖ Leicester Square

It's brash, it's bright and it's brilliant value, even if they don't offer the speediest or friendliest service. The portions here are wonderfully generous and of freshly prepared, but don't ask for any alterations to the menu or you risk being strung up with the tormented-looking ducks above the cookers. This is a café that is loud and cheap (though not particularly cheerful), and for a late-night snack it sure beats 'meat and chips' from a greasy kebab shop round a windy street corner.

◉ *Mon–Sat, 11.30am–11pm*

◐ *Seafood with noodles, £5*

◕ *£2.50 per glass*

New Piccadilly Café

8 Denman Street, W1

(020) 7437 8530

⊖ Piccadilly Circus

An old-fashioned treat for Londoners and tourists alike – in an age overrun by Starbucks, Nero and Costa this is a bastion of the 1950s formica-clad coffee shop of old. Even the menu has hardly changed for half a century and one half-expects to see the poets and writers who frequented Soho in years gone by to be quietly scribbling away in a corner. You'll be charged a mere 60 pence for a cup of coffee, and when was the last time you paid that little for anything in Central London?

◉ *Depends what the manager was doing the night before*

◐ *Sausage, egg and chips, £4.50*

Central

LEICESTER SQUARE RESTAURANTS

Aberdeen Angus Steakhouse
20 Cranbourne Street, WC2
(020) 7836 3782
⊖ Leicester Square

For a prime (rib) example of where not to end up at 11pm when you're so smashed you can barely stand up, look no further than this timeless illustration of London dining at its worst. It's overpriced and to be quite honest, the food is barely better than at McDonald's – but only because it's served on a plate.

🕒 *Mon–Wed, 11.30am–11pm;*
Thu–Sat, 11.30am–11.30pm
🍴 *New York sirloin steak, £16.50*
💷 *£12.50*

Gaucho Grill
25 Swallow Street, W1
(020) 7734 4040
⊖ Piccadilly Circus

If all you're dreaming of is a man-sized steak to make you feel like Desperate Dan on a bender, then come here. This is a sumptuous hideaway just off Piccadilly Circus and is not to be missed. This taste of Argentina will get you wanting to hop on a jet to Buenos Aires pronto. Don't miss the empanadas (posh pasties) as a starter. The staff really do know their rumps from their rib eyes and it's worth chatting to them about their indulgent menus.

🕒 *Mon–Fri, 12pm–11.30pm; Sat, 12pm–*
12am; Sun, 12pm–10.30pm
🍴 *Gaucho burger, £13*
💷 *£18.50*

Experience
118 Shaftsbury Avenue, W1
(020) 7437 0377
⊖ Leicester Square

Between noon and 5pm you'll probably have to queue for a table, wait for the next ice age to catch a waitress' eye, be uncomfortably close to other diners, and probably deafened by them, but you must try this place. Experience offers half price dim sum everyday before 5pm and most of them are exquisite. Unsurprisingly, it's not very veggie-friendly but there are a couple of veg-only mains and dim sum available. Tasty food at tasty prices.

🕒 *Mon–Fri, 12pm–11pm; Sat, 12pm–*
11.30pm; Sun, 12pm–10.30pm
🍴 *Shredded pork with noodles, £3.80*
💷 *175ml glass, £3.50*

Kettners
29 Romilly Street, W1
(020) 7734 6112
⊖ Leicester Square

Probably Britain's poshest pizza and burger restaurant. The flagship in the mighty Pizza Express chain, Kettners exudes class, from its palatial carpets and gleaming chandeliers to its starched white tablecloths and tinkling grand piano. While pizzas are the mainstay of the menu you'll also find pasta, grills and salads, together with an impressive wine and champagne list. It's buzzy, sophisticated and entirely unpretentious. Luxury was never so pleasingly affordable.

🕒 *Mon–Sun, 11am–1am*
🍴 *Kettners special burger, £9.95*
💷 *£14.95*

Questo

26 Romilly Street, W1
(020) 7287 5681
⊖ Leicester Square

Itchy is very pro-buffet. You can gorge yourself with exactly what your stomach desires without having to cunningly hide sprouts and the like under a blanket of mashed potato. Questo, however, is an über-buffet of pure foody joy. It serves tasty Italian grub at rock bottom prices while waiters float around proffering trays of goodies, so it's no longer even necessary to leave your seat. Better still, there's no need to book, so pop down before sampling some of Soho's drinking establishments.

🕒 *Mon–Sun, 12pm–10.30pm*
🍴 *Buffet, £5.80 before 6pm, £7.50 after*
💰 *£9.90*

St Moritz

159 Wardour Street, W1
(020) 7437 0525
⊖ Oxford Circus/Tottenham Court Road

If you're one of those people who laugh in the face of the dessert trolley and head straight for the cheese plate, you've just found your private slice of heaven – or your Garden of Edam, if you will. In the middle of bustling Wardour Street stands a tiny little ski chalet, (or what looks like one), and hiding behind its doors the best pots of stinky, drippy, flavoursome fondue that's ever crossed your breadbasket.

🕒 *Mon–Fri, 12pm–3pm & 6pm–11.30pm;*
Sat, 6pm–11.30pm
🍴 *Fondue forestiere with wild mushrooms and cubes of bread, £14.90 per person*
💰 *£13.95*

Satsuma

56 Wardour Street, W1
(020) 7437 8338
⊖ Piccadilly Circus

A classier Wagamama, Satsuma is a large Japanese restaurant with minimalist décor and bench seating. Pricier than its rival, the portions are much more sizeable. Bento boxes are a nifty all-in-one solution if you're indecisive, while miso soup comes as a side with most dishes. It's also open until midnight over the weekend – the gauntlet has been thrown.

🕒 *Mon–Tue, 12pm–11pm; Wed–Thu,*
12pm–11.30pm; Fri–Sat, 12pm–12am;
Sun, 12pm–10.30pm
🍴 *Satsuma bento, £15.90;*
mixed sashimi, £9.90
💰 *£13*

Zilli Fish

36–40 Brewer Street, W1
(020) 7734 8649
⊖ Piccadilly Circus

You might remember him for his attempts on *X Factor* but don't hold that against him – Aldo Zilli's food is much better than his falsetto. Seafood-based with a bit of pasta and risotto thrown in, working your way through the menu you'll even get a grasp of the Italian language. How about 'Gamberoni, aglio e olio bruschetta' – that's tiger prawns, garlic and oil served on bruschetta to us. Or you could just have mushroom risotto.

🕒 *Mon–Sat, 12pm–11.30pm*
🍴 *Seared tuna steak with*
Niçoise salad, £19
💰 *£16.50*

Central

CHARING CROSS

Exotika

7 Villiers Street, WC2

(020) 7930 6133

⊖ Charing Cross/Embankment

Surprisingly this is not a dodgy massage parlour but a fusion café with a nice selection of light and healthy meals. Minimalist walls and high stools make it feel like a cross between a school canteen and a *Dr Who* set, but with candles and down-tempo tunes you'll be relaxing in no time. The food's served promptly and despite that just-been-nuked-feel, is pretty darn tasty, and as cheap as a Bernard Manning gag.

🄯 *Mon–Sat, 11am–11pm; Sun, 12pm–10pm*

🄯 *Beef fajitas with rice, £5.95*

🄯 *BYO, £1 corkage*

The Harp

47 Chandos Place, WC2

(020) 7836 0291

⊖ Charing Cross

Forget your Wetherspoons and Slug-and-mouldy-Lettuce pub-a-likes, this is the real deal. Teeny tiny old-fashioned pub near Trafalgar Square complete with wrinkly men who've been there for so long they're practically growing out the floor. Truly stunning stained glass windows, weirdly cool oil paintings, and real ales, Guinness and various sausage sarnies to die for. Gets surprisingly busy, considering how the masses are usually allergic to pubs without Balsamic vinegar somewhere on view, so get there early to beat the codgers.

🄯 *Mon–Sat, 11am–11pm; Sun, 11am–10.30pm; Food, Mon–Sun, 12pm–3pm*

GREEN PARK

The Golden Lion

25 King Street, SW1

(020) 7925 0007

⊖ Piccadilly Circus/Green Park

After hours of scrubbing it up with Brasso you hurry down to Christie's to get that 18th century Harrison marine watch that your granddad left you valued, only to find it's a fake. Next stop, a pint in The Golden Lion over the road to drown your sorrows. This is a lovely pub with a lot of history, a theatrical theme throughout and some artefacts from the old St James' Theatre. There's also a decent selection of real ale, Sky TV for sports and a choice of smoking or non-smoking rooms.

🄯 *Mon–Fri, 11am–11pm; Sat, 12pm–8pm*

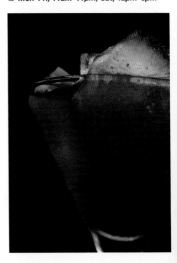

HOLBORN

Bar Polski

11 Little Turnstile, WC1

(020) 7831 9679

⊖ Holborn

Not much has changed since Na Zdrowie became Bar Polski, and it's still one of the best places to start your essential education into the world of vodka. There are over 50 kinds here which they recommend you treat as a kind of browsing menu, shot style (vodka tapas – now there's a concept). Fortunately there is also hearty Polish nosh to help you remain vertical.

Ⓒ Mon, 4pm–11pm; Tue–Fri, 12.30pm–11pm; Sat, 6pm–11pm; Food, 'til 10pm

Ⓘ Meat stew and sauerkraut, £6.60

Ⓩ £10.50

Guanabara

Parker Street, WC2

(020) 7242 8600

⊖ Holborn/Covent Garden

Close your eyes and let the rhythm of the samba and the sweet taste of cachaça flow. A vivacious music venue playing samba and funk beats until the early hours; Guanabara even offers free evenings of live Brazilian jazz and sounds to entice the most reluctant feet onto the dance floor. And with 34 varieties of cachaça, Latino beers, exotic fruit caipirinhas and a Brazilian menu there are no excuses for not having an Amazon time.

Ⓒ Mon–Sat, 5pm–2.30am; Sun, 5pm–12am

Ⓘ Feijoadinha – Brazilian pork & black bean stew with rice & farofa, £6

Ⓩ £13.50

The George

213 The Strand, WC2

(020) 7353 9667

⊖ Temple

Founded in 1723, this is one of the Strand's oldest pubs, and back in the day you could have rubbed shoulders with regulars such as the con man Henry Perfect, who apparently impersonated vicars. It has recently been tastefully refurbished, unlike many other traditional London boozers which have poncified out of all recognition, and with the Royal Courts of Justice opposite it's the perfect place to celebrate your freedom with its hearty selection of pub grub. Perhaps a King George burger and a drop of London Pride. A fine old pub.

Ⓒ Mon–Thu, 11am–11.30pm; Fri–Sat, 11am–12am; Sun, 12pm–7pm

Old Crown

33 New Oxford Street, WC1

(020) 7836 9121

⊖ Holborn/Tottenham Court Road

This formerly rather elegant pub has had a typical 'noughties' makeover. Now complete with de rigueur wooden tables and a serious, 'we are a gastropub' interior, it's actually rather a good find. The food is hearty at lunch and shifts to meze-style sharing plates in the evening, making it appealing for after-work drinks. As expected, the wine is carefully sourced – doesn't anywhere these days serve a good warm Liebfraumilch?

Ⓒ Sun–Wed, 12pm–12am; Thu–Sat, 12pm–2am; Food, 12pm–10pm

Ⓘ Prime Argentinian rib-eye with Café de Paris butter, £10.95

Ⓩ £11.50

Central

MARYLEBONE

The Globe Tavern
43–47 Marylebone Road, NW1
(020) 7935 6368
☻ Baker Street

After three centuries you'd hope they'd have got it right. And they have – the Globe is a break from the bars scattered around here. It gets quite busy with creative cliques early evening but there's plenty of room outside if it gets packed. Good for people watching, and serves excellent fish and chips. Get battered in every glorious sense of the word.

☻ Mon–Fri, 11am–11pm; Sat, 11am–11.30pm; Sun, 11am–10.30pm; Food, Mon–Sat, 12pm–10pm; Sun, 12pm–9pm
🍴 Fish and chips, £6.50
💰 £11.50

Suze in Mayfair
41 North Audley Street, W1
(020) 7491 3237
☻ Marble Arch

There are quite a few Antipodean chefs working the capital with their g'day-mate grins and menus full of chooks and crocs, but none seems to do it for down under quite like Suze. This family-run restaurant has been around for almost eight years and is staffed by the prettiest, friendliest Australasian bunch you'll ever meet. Itchy loves the mammoth green-lipped mussels and the perfectly cooked lamb, which falls off your fork and bleats until you've eaten every last morsel.

☻ Mon–Sat, 11am–11pm
🍴 Three course meal, around £40
💰 £11.95

RIBA Café
66 Portland Place, W1
(020) 7631 0467
☻ Great Portland Street

Bit of a posh one this. Head here for your pan-fried calf's liver and for the terrace, which is where the proverbial 'it' is at for lunch in the summer. Being on the first floor of the Royal Institute of British Architects you know you're in for some interesting company, should you head to this well-priced coffee bar and brasserie alone. Just remember that an aptitude for extravagant Lego and Meccano creations at age six does not mean you should launch into your thoughts on the construction business. Keep it real and tuck into a toastie.

☻ Mon–Fri, 8am–6pm; Sat, 9am–4pm
🍴 Average lunch, £10

EDGWARE ROAD

Colbeh
6 Porchester Place, W2
(020) 7706 4888
☻ Marble Arch

A tiny restaurant that serves Persian cuisine in trencherman portions but with a refined and delicate hand. The mosaic-covered tandoori oven bakes the doughy naan-like bread that you use to mop up your starter meze, before moving onto mains spiked with walnuts, pomegranates and chilli, which make for a rich and luscious repast. The best bit is that it's cheap, cheap, cheap: £3 for starters and around £8 for a main.

☻ Mon–Sun, 12pm–11.30pm
🍴 Stew of kings, £8.90
💰 BYO

Oh my cod

'PLAICE PLEASE ME', SANG THE BEATLES. OBVIOUSLY THEY FOUND IT TRICKY TO FIND A DECENT CHIPPY ONCE THEY MOVED TO THE CAPITAL. IF ONLY THEY'D READ THE ITCHY GUIDE TO LONDON CHIPPIES

Fryer's Delight
19 Theobald's Road, WC1
(020) 7405 4114
⊖ Holborn

Not one for non-meat eaters – everything here is lovingly cooked in veggie-offending beef dripping. Luckily, this place's 50s authenticity means it won't take them long to wipe the blood off the formica tables when you're punched in the face by an angry cow lover. Still, we'd take this joint over our own personal safety any day.

🕒 *Mon–Sat, 12pm–10pm*

The Golden Hind
73 Marylebone Lane, W1
(020) 7486 3644
⊖ Bond Street

Mmmm. We love that wholesome, deep-fried goodness. The Golden Hind does fish and chips the way they should be done. From the perfect-every-time batter to the homemade tartare sauce, this is probably where the angels come for lunch on a Friday, if they can get a table.

🕒 *Mon–Fri, 12pm–3pm & 6pm–10pm; Sat, 6pm–10pm*

Fish Central
149–151 Central Street, EC1
(020) 7253 4970
⊖ Old Street

Ignore the housing-estate location, and walk in to what looks like a swanky restaurant. Except for the prices, this is about as far away from swanky food as you're going to get, though. There's loadsa types of fish, 'real' chips, mushy peas, and scampi for the lady. Propah.

🕒 *Mon–Thu, 11am–2.30pm & 5pm–10.30pm; Fri–Sat, 11am–2.30pm & 5pm–11pm*

Masters Super Fish
191 Waterloo Road, SE1
(020) 7928 6924
⊖ Waterloo

It's not in the nicest location (well, it is near Waterloo), but with fish fresh shipped in daily from Billingsgate Fish Market, this is the plaice to get your sole-food. But be warned – the portions are so hefty that you may want to file for a-salt and batter-y.

🕒 *Mon, 5.30pm–10.30pm; Tue–Thu & Sat, 12pm–3pm & 4.30pm–10.30pm; Fri, 4.30pm–11pm*

North vs South

BACK IN 1666, AS THE GREAT FIRE OF LONDON BLAZED ACROSS THE RIVER, THE GOOD FOLK OF SOUTH LONDON LOOKED ON, GRINNING, WITH A JOVIAL EVENING PINT. AND NOT A LOT HAS CHANGED SINCE THEN REALLY

Tribal rivalry is an essential part of our culture. You only have to look at the way Southerners are scornfully labelled as 'fairies' by the 'monkeys' north of the Watford Gap, or how warring football firms make dates to thrash each other with bike chains in NCP car parks.

London has seen all kinds of squabbling factions come and go, but even in this modern age of tolerance and empathy, the great divide of the Thames remains as strong as ever. South Londoners complain that their dull Northern neighbours look down on them, failing to appreciate the enormous diversity and excitement of their districts, while North Londoners make snide remarks about the appropriate clothing for a night south of the river being a Challenger II tank.

All this is nothing new. Centuries ago, when the only connection with the South Bank was the old London Bridge (closing at dusk) and a couple of ferrymen, the Northerners made similar remarks about the seedy but artistic Bankside district, and the residents of that area had the last laugh a few years later when fire reduced much of the north bank to a scale model of Dot Cotton's ashtray.

These days, as with almost everything else, the great North/South London competition has become a marketing tool. In 2006, thousands turned up to Nike's Run London event, and Seb Coe's orange-clad Southerners beat Paula Radcliffe's green-vested Northerners over the 10k run. It looks like South London may have the upper hand for now, but there's always the next one in October…

North

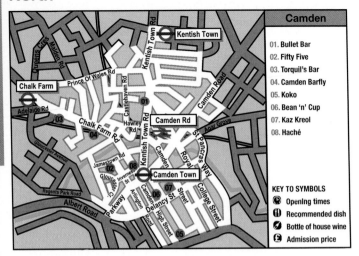

Camden

01. Bullet Bar
02. Fifty Five
03. Torquil's Bar
04. Camden Barfly
05. Koko
06. Bean 'n' Cup
07. Kaz Kreol
08. Haché

KEY TO SYMBOLS

@ Opening times
@ Recommended dish
@ Bottle of house wine
@ Admission price

CAMDEN BARS

Bullet Bar

147 Kentish Town Road, NW1
(020) 7485 6040
⊖ Camden Town/Kentish Town

It wouldn't be funny to call a bar this if it were located in Hackney, but being in Camden the clientele don't come in sporting Kevlar. We could lounge for hours in this top notch cocktail spot, but we can't afford to. In summer the huge roof garden is the place to pull, or just eye up the meeja types and totty in strapless numbers. Does great tapas too, so if we were you, we'd be there in a (hem hem) shot.

@ *Mon–Wed, 5pm–12am; Thu, 5pm–1am;*
Fri–Sat, 4pm–1am; Sun, 3pm–12am
@ *£14.50*

Fifty Five

31 Jamestown Road, NW1
(020) 7424 9054
⊖ Camden Town

MC Grammar, Itchy's rad rapping English teacher, taught us that the word 'recuperative' is an anagram of 'cue pervert, ai'. Clearly, this means that doing anything to try and recover from a hangover is twisted and wrong. Pure souls keep drinking. Here. The Fifty Five boys run pretty much the best cocktail bar we've found in London, and are close to god-like. The 160-plus drinks are expertly spun, juggled and flambéed into existence with circus-standard flair, all your favourite house party tunes play, everyone is greeted like a regular, and cocktails are 2-for-1 every day, 6pm–8pm. FF-ing brilliant.

@ *Mon–Sun, 5pm–12.30am*

Gilgamesh Babylon Lounge

The Stables, Chalk Farm Road, NW1

(020) 7482 5757

⊖ Camden Town

We love that this is open late, but for the damage a drink here'll do to your earnings, you may as well go on *Celeb Big Brother* and act all racist. So chances are you can't afford to stay all night anyway. The adjoining restaurant generated a lot of hype last summer, but the food's highly overrated, so save your pennies for another cocktail in this carved tavern of wonder. From the shiny mirrors to the massive bar, to the totally gorgeous (if obnoxious) bar staff, this is one for a seriously special occasion.

🕒 *Tue–Sat, 6pm–2.30am; Sun, 6pm–1.30am*

🍴 *Tea-smoked trout, £9.50*

💰 *£13*

The Proud Gallery

Gin House, Stables Market, Chalk Farm Road, NW1

(020) 7482 3867

⊖ Chalk Farm/Camden Town

This famous North London photographic art gallery did us a favour and installed a bar on the roof. Well, actually, it's more of a glorified marquee, which makes it more suitable for summer soirées, but as it's located in grotty Camden, we like it all year round. Exhibitions mean that this place allows you the fun of enjoying a beer while trying to identify the sweaty man with long hair in one of the many photos hanging on the walls. They hold the odd gig on the other part of the roof. By the way, the sweaty man with long hair turned out to be Madonna. Blame it on the Corona.

🕒 *Mon–Sun, 11am–6pm*

💰 *£12*

Positively 4th Street

119 Hampstead Road, NW1

(020) 7388 5380

⊖ Warren Street

Okay, so it's not really in Camden, but it's close, alright? The crusties in Camden'd never appreciate such a cool American style bar and its tasty Japanese food, anyway. The high ceilings and the retro yet sexy décor make you feel a little like you're sitting on the Lower East side of New York City, and regular DJ nights make staying late a treat. Ladies, get a bloke to buy you a banana crème cocktail, preferably using the line 'Is that the money for a banana crème cocktail in your pocket, or are you just pleased to see me?'

🕒 *Mon–Thu, 12pm–3pm & 5pm–11pm; Fri, 12pm–1am; Sat, 7pm–1am*

🍴 *Japanese cosmopolitan, £4.50*

Torquil's Bar & Terrace

1st Floor Roundhouse, Chalk Farm Road, NW1

(0870) 389 9920

⊖ Chalk Farm

Thank God they re-did the Roundhouse, because it's fast becoming one of Itchy's fave places. If you haven't got tickets to the latest play, performance or gig, you can still hang out in its glorious confines for some top notch-food and drink. In the summer Torquil's rooftop is packed with BBQ-munching groups of friends, lounging on the steps, listening to music. A relatively secret slice of London greatness that we reckon'll probably catch on quick.

🕒 *Mon, 12pm–5.30pm; Tue–Sat, 12pm–11pm; Sun, 12pm–7pm*

🍴 *Roundhouse burger, £9.50*

💰 *£12*

North

CAMDEN PUBS

The Cuban

Stables Market, Chalk Farm Road, NW1

(020) 7424 0692

⊖ Camden Town/Chalk Farm

It's big, it's brash and it's usually filled with tourists rifling through their bags of market clobber and exclaiming that they've just scored a bargain. That is, of course, before ordering an overpriced burger to go with their overpriced pint. It's not the cheapest place to stop, especially when the surrounding food stalls have filled our tummies for a lot less, but it's lively, fun and funky, so it scores a mention anyway.

☺ *Mon–Thu, 10am–1am; Fri–Sat,*
10am–2am; Sun, 10am–12am
🍴 *Tapas, from £4*

The Hawley Arms

2 Castlehaven Road, NW1

(020) 7428 5979

⊖ Camden Town/Kentish Town

Oi, celeb spotters! Get ye here if you're after finding some big-name sleb slumming it. Not far from the MTV studios, you're quite likely to find yourself sitting next to an A-list escapee in here. Or alternatively, some jaded producer looking for the next big thing. If you wanna make it, waltz up to the bar, ignore the range of great grub and drink, and burst forth into warbly song to order a Diet Coke. Or, you could prove your star credentials by heading to the roof terrace and threatening to chuck yourself off if you don't get an audition.

☺ *Mon–Thu & Sun, 12pm–12am;*
Fri–Sat, 12pm–1am
✪ *£11.50*

The Good Mixer

30 Inverness Street, NW1

(020) 7916 6176

⊖ Camden Town

Back in the day this boozer was the epicentre of Britpop's social scene. Yep, all the greats hung out here: Blur, Elastica, erm... Menswear. Ok, so it's hardly the coolest claim to fame, but the joint's got history, and it still plays host to all manner of rock 'n' roll raconteurs, for all you indie anoraks whose musical tastes haven't evolved since '96. And you're about the only people who are going to want to head here. It smells worse than Shaun Ryder's kecks after a 30 date tour, and has the same attention paid to the interior décor as Noel Gallagher gave to writing meaningful lyrics.

☺ *Mon–Sat, 12pm–1am; Sun, 1pm–12.30pm*
✪ *£12.50*

Oh! Bar

111–113 Camden High Street, NW1

(020) 7383 0330

⊖ Camden Town/Mornington Crescent

It's a funny one this – it's like your favourite old student bar. The one with all the seedy dark corners and the DJ who loved himself, as well as the line of sickly alco-pops behind the bar that you know you shouldn't touch but do anyway. Everything about this weirdly-shaped bar will make you wonder why you're in here, but you still won't want to leave. There's something about that circular dance floor, too. If you're not shaking yo' bad thang in the middle of it, someone else will be, so you might as well get yourself in there first.

☺ *Sun–Wed, 12pm–12am; Thu–Sat, 12pm–2am*
✪ *£12*

CAMDEN CLUBS

Camden Barfly

49 Chalk Farm Road, NW1

(020) 7916 1049

⊖ Camden Town/Chalk Farm

They might only serve Worthington bitter at three quid a pint, but hey, it's where you are that matters. Even after all these years we still can't get enough of this place. We love its mixed crowd, ranging from fresh-faced students to old-time locals, plus the live music scene here's pretty much where it's at for discovering up-and-coming bands – anyone who's anyone plays here during the early stages of their career. Proper indie grooving at its best. We hope it never changes.

☻ *Opening hours vary, call to check*

Purple Turtle

65 Crowndale Road, NW1

(020) 7383 4976

⊖ Mornington Crescent

The truth is, if you can't get into Koko for whatever reason, you're probably going to end up here. It's practically opposite the place, and in spite of the doorman who gets his kicks from being rather large and scary, once you're in you can breathe a sigh of relief. It mightn't be the coolest venue in the world – you have to dodge the snogging students at weekends and occasionally the place has an air of festering puke – but if you're after reliving your students' union days to a range of rock bands, you could do an awful lot worse than head here.

☻ *Mon–Thu, 12pm–12am; Fri–Sat, 12pm–2am; Sun, 12pm–12am*

Koko

1a Camden High Street, NW1

(08704) 432 5527

⊖ Mornington Crescent

Alongside relatively new openings Gilgamesh and the Roundhouse, this opulently trendy venue is at the forefront of the wave of places chic-ing up Camden. North London's royal palace for all things musical's weekly club nights are so popular that the back of the queue is usually in Euston. Friday nights see an excellent selection of music and live bands, but turn up late and you'll find yourself at the back of that queue, then you'll pretty much be halfway home already.

☻ *Admission and opening times vary depending on the event, but usually early evening until very late and £5–£8 admission*

North

CAMDEN CAFÉS

Bean 'n' Cup
104 Camden High Street, NW1
(020) 7267 7340
⊖ Camden

If you're after hot food, this isn't the ideal place, as the most substantial the food here gets is a range of sandwiches. However, this High Street café is so cosy you could curl up here for hours with one their seasonal teas and a cake or two. As well as being a very nice place to spend an hour with a newspaper in some warming surroundings, the Bean 'n' Cup also sells a selection of gifts such as novelty tea pots and clocks. Great smoothies in the summer and special cups of char in the winter.

🍴 Sandwiches, £1.99–£2.75

Cow and Coffee Bean
The Broadwalk, Chester Road, Regents Park, NW1
(020) 7224 3872
⊖ Baker Street/Regent's Park

Remember when you were little and you went crazy over that tub of Nesquik, because you didn't know any better? Well you can't change the past (unless of course you've got a mad scientist friend and enough room to get a DeLorean up to 88 miles an hour), but you can change your milkshake-drinking future. The shakes in this Regent's Park kiosk are all made with milk from real farm moo-cows, and so is the ice-cream. Even the kids with their creamy grins won't bother you, 'cause you'll feel like one yourself.

🕒 *Mon–Sun, summer, 9am–8pm;*
Mon–Sun, winter, 10am–3pm
🍴 *Sandwiches, £2.25–£3.95*

CAMDEN RESTAURANTS

Arizona Bar and Grill

2a Jamestown Road, NW1

(020) 7284 4730

🚇 Camden Town

This mammoth restaurant just round the corner from Camden market continues to puzzle us, because we're not sure that it even knows what it is. The cocktails are Mexican enough, the food is averagely South American, but the venue and the people who eat in it make the place feel more like a Wimpy bar for grown-ups. Very strange. Still, good for a hen night – there are always a few on weekends.

🕒 *Mon–Thu, 11am–12am; Fri–Sat, 11am–1.30am; Sun, 11am–12am*

🍴 *BBQ ribs, £9.95*

Haché

24 Inverness Street, NW1

(020) 7485 9100

🚇 Camden Town

This family-run burger restaurant has won just about every award going for its excellent ground beef creations, and despite the fact that these supposedly gourmet burger joints are popping up all over the place, it's not hard to see why. Trust us on this, what with the friendly service, relaxed but classy atmosphere and excellent cooking, you will not find a finer burger anywhere in London. Numerous veggie, chicken and fish burgers are also available, so if you're out for a burger and you don't end up here, then Ha-shame on you.

🕒 *Mon–Sat, 12pm–10.30pm; Sun, 12pm–10pm*

🍴 *Steak Spanish burger, £7.95*

💷 *£9.95*

Green Note

106 Parkway, NW1

(020) 7485 9899

🚇 Camden Town

They're a bit of a jack of all trades this lot. Not only do they run a vegetarian restaurant here, but they also find time to operate a live music venue out of the same premises. Since opening in 2005 this has been a hit with visitors and locals alike, and the no-smoking restaurant at the front cleverly capitalises on the mob mentality of the public when it comes to smoking. There's a funky bar at the back, and the international tapas here are a real forte, too.

🕒 *Tue–Fri, 6pm–11pm; Sat, 12pm–11pm; Sun, 12pm–10.30pm*

🍴 *Mock duck, spring onion and cucumber spring rolls served with hoisin sauce, £3.95*

Kaz Kreol

35 Pratt Street, NW1

(020) 7485 4747

🚇 Camden Town/Mornington Crescent

If you long for the heat of the Seychelles, or you've been and want another taste, this little beauty aims to please by offering a host of traditional grub with an emphasis on fish and seafood. With its modern décor and black granite tables, it's authentic, tasty enough to warrant the price, and means that the closest you get to the Seychelles in London isn't hearing a mini-skirted Leicester Square oompah-loompah's bleat of 'Say 'Chelle, you shouldn't have drunk them breezers so quick' to a vomiting mate.

🕒 *Mon–Sat, 12pm–3.30pm & 7pm–11pm*

🍴 *Meal for two with wine, £50*

💷 *£9.95*

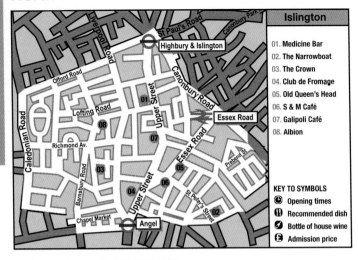

Islington

01. Medicine Bar
02. The Narrowboat
03. The Crown
04. Club de Fromage
05. Old Queen's Head
06. S & M Café
07. Galipoli Café
08. Albion

KEY TO SYMBOLS
- Opening times
- Recommended dish
- Bottle of house wine
- Admission price

(Map labels: Liverpool Road, St Paul's Road, Canonbury Park, Highbury & Islington, Offord Road, Canonbury Road, Lofting Road, Upper Street, Essex Road, Caledonian Road, Richmond Av., Essex Road, Barnsbury Road, Prebend St., Chapel Market, Upper Street, St Peter's Street, Angel)

ISLINGTON BARS

Clockwork

66–68 Pentonville Road, N1
(020) 7837 5387
Angel

Itchy and our droogs popped down here for a bit of the old ultra-violence, with the intention of getting blitzed on drug-laced milk and listening to some rousing Ludwig Van. What we found was a funky DJ bar with crazy lighting, melty sofas and a programme of music spread over two floors. The cocktails were delicious, and the whole experience had Itchy's droogs a malenky bit poogly. They decided that bedways was rightways, but Itchy decided barways was betterways. Anyway, the punters loved our eye makeup.

Times vary

Keston Lodge

131 Upper Street, N1
(020) 7354 9535
Angel/Highbury and Islington

A faux-boho joint that attracts the masses rather than gangs of unwashed, scurvy-ridden wannabe poets. From the leather sofas to the spoons on the wall, Keston Lodge is where people go to pretend they're down with the kids. DJs avoid luring in the hordes by steering clear of house, but that doesn't mean this place doesn't crowd please when it comes to mixing up decent cocktails. Prices are strictly for adults though – if you want to relive your rebellious youth, there are newsagents selling White Lightning nearby.

Mon–Wed, 12pm–12am; Thu, 12am–1am; Fri–Sat, 12pm–2am; Sun, 12am–11.30pm
£13.50

Medicine Bar

181 Upper Street, N1

(020) 7704 8056

⊖ Highbury and Islington

The comfy curve of sofas at the back just beckons for a second date snuggle or a loud group of mates swigging bottles of cheap beer. During the day it's dark as well as being slightly grubby, but at night, when the DJ's spinning and the seats are spilling over with laughing Islingtonites drinking cocktails, that's when the party really gets started. It's pretty packed on weekends, but it's always a great place to stop on that obligatory Upper Street pub crawl.

ⓒ *Mon–Thu, 5pm–12am; Fri, 3pm–2am; Sat, 12pm–2am; Sun, 12pm–10.30pm*

ⓐ *Fri–Sat after 10pm, £4*

ⓐ *Mon–Fri, £6.95 'til 9pm; Sat–Sun, £11.95*

ISLINGTON PUBS

Albion

10 Thornhill Road, N1

(020) 7607 7450

⊖ Highbury and Islington/Angel

Strolling through the back streets of Barnsbury can feel a bit like you've somehow stepped back in time to provincial Sussex, circa 1927, and stumbling across the Albion does little to dispel this. Behind its village pub frontage, what appears to be quite a small bar keeps stretching round corners into more and more rooms, with lovely beer gardens at front and back. If you're lucky you might catch Poirot sitting in a corner exercising ze little grey cells on his latest widowcide while Hastings prances round like a tool in motoring goggles.

ⓒ *Mon–Sat; 11am–11pm; Sun, 12pm–10.30pm*

The Narrowboat

119 St Peters Street, N1

(020) 7288 0572

⊖ Angel

Let us know if you disagree, but we at Itchy believe that there's no better way to spend an evening than sitting by a canal, drinking bottles of fizzy cider, happily burping away as the boats putter up and down before us. Which explains why The Narrowboat is the apple of our eye when it comes to waterside boozing. Come summer or winter (they have nice big windows to keep the weather out), this is one for getting out of your box before making a pledge to buy a boat of your own one day.

ⓒ *Mon–Sat, 11am–12am; Sun, 12pm–12am. Food, Mon–Fri, 12pm–3pm & 5pm–9.30pm; Sat–Sun, 12pm–9.30pm*

ⓐ *£11.50*

North

The Crown

116 Cloudesley Road, N1

⊖ Angel

(020) 7837 7107

We have an old saying at Itchy: 'There are pubs, there are gastropubs and then there's The Crown'. Tucked away safely away from the marauding chav armies of Upper Street, there's a sunny beer garden for cheeky summer lunchtime halves, an open fire to warm your toes in winter and good grub to stuff your face with all year round. The prices may not be as smart as your average boozer – you wouldn't get much for a crown in here – but then you get what you pay for, and everything about this place is top dollar.

◉ *Mon–Sat, 12pm–11pm; Sun, 12pm–10.30pm; Food, Mon–Fri, 12pm–3pm & 6pm–10pm; Sat, 12pm–10pm; Sun, 12pm–9pm*

Filthy McNasty's

68 Amwell Street, EC1

⊖ Angel

(020) 7837 6067

We've never met him, but however rancid and rude Mr McNasty might be, he sure as hell knows how to run a bar. If you fancy getting smashed with the likes of Shane Pogue and Pete Libertine-Babyshamble, you'll find them here in between what you'd hope were trips to rooms full of hot water and soap. Not that we're just into stargazing, but if knocking back pints of Red Stripe is good enough for them, it's bloody well good enough for us. Although this is where we draw the line at imitating their antics. We like our teeth.

◉ *Mon–Sat, 12pm–11pm; Sun, 12pm–10.30pm; Food, Mon–Fri, 12pm–3pm*

◉ £12.50

King's Head

115 Upper Street, N1

⊖ Angel

(020) 7226 3443

A London entertainment hall in the greatest of traditions. Out back is a little theatre where, when they haven't got a show on, you can lounge with your pint among the faded red velvet furnishings. Itchy loves this place for the late opening hours and their commitment to putting on live music every night. The last three times we've been in, we've seen a klezmer group, a jazz ensemble and a brass band, complete with sousaphone. Which comes a close second to the Bolivian armpit flute for most hilarious instrument in history.

◉ *Mon–Thu, 11am–1am; Fri–Sat, 11am–2am; Sun, 12pm–12.30am*

◉ £13

ISLINGTON CLUBS

Club de Fromage @ Bar Academy

16 Parkfield Street, N1

(020) 7288 4400

⊖ Angel

Take a healthy measure of Brian Potter, mix with a dose of Peter Stringfellow, and add a playlist that students' union DJs across the nation dream of, and you have this night. Run by Fat Tony and his son, Slow Alfie, the steady stream of dour Northern banter from the stage is interrupted only by a meat pie raffle, a set from air guitar band Lucifer's Grandmother, and the dancefloor exploding as the DJs drop another pop classic. Genius.

© Sat, 10pm–4am

€ £5 before 12am/NUS, £7 after

The Old Queen's Head

44 Essex Road, N1

(020) 7354 9993

⊖ Angel

The Old Queen's Head has had quite a year of it. They've not only had a huge makeover, they've also become a DJ pub (DJ bars are so 2006, darling, now it's all about comfy pubs hosting the kind of DJs you usually have to pay club prices to see), which basically means that you've now got to pay three quid to get past the doorman at weekends. Still, the place hosts the likes of the Plump DJs and Joe Ransom for next to nothing, which is good news for anyone who doesn't fancy joining the crush on Fabric's dancefloor.

© Mon–Wed, 12pm–12am; Thu, 12pm–1am; Fri–Sat, 12pm–2am; Sun, 12pm–11pm

North

ISLINGTON CAFÉS

Art to Zen
27 Upper Street, N1
(020) 7226 5300
⊖ Angel

This cute little coffee shop attracts the Islingtonites mid-shopping with its chilled live music, local art, and of course, that tempting aroma of freshly brewed coffee. We always wonder what else these people put in those pots to make it smell so inviting. Get a tasty little snack whipped up in your honour to enjoy while you wait for your mates to show up. It's also a great spot for the Sunday papers if your flatmate's hogging the sofa for *Hollyoaks*.

🕒 Mon–Sun, 10.30am–11pm
🍴 *Three course Japanese lunch, £8.95*

S & M Café
4–6 Essex Road, N1
(020) 7359 5361
⊖ Angel

The thing Itchy loves about this place is the awkward look on people's faces when we say we're going to the S & M Café. After letting them flounder for a minute, when we explain that it's a sausage and mash café, the relief is palpable. Serving an array of gourmet sausages and a variety of mashes, feel free to mix and mash (oh yes) your choices, then sit back and be proud of Britain. This place makes life worth living.

🕒 Mon–Thu, 7.30am–11.30pm; Fri,
7.30am–12am; Sat, 8.30am–12am;
Mon, 8.30am–10.30pm
🍴 *Two sausages, mash and gravy, £5.95*
🍷 *£10.95*

Candid Arts Café
3 Torrens Street, EC1
(020) 7837 4237
⊖ Angel

Tucked away behind Islington High Street and above the Candid Arts Gallery, this is the definition of a 'find'. About as far from Costa Coffee as you can get in a café, Candid Arts is shabby chic at its best, with worn old armchairs, a massive communal dining table, dripping candles, and shelves of board game compendiums. Be warned, though – a 'friendly' game of Snakes & Ladders can rumble the foundations of even the most solid friendship. But who needs friends when winning's at stake?

🕒 Mon–Sat, 12pm–10pm; Sun, 12pm–5pm
🍴 *Chocolate fudge cake with cream, £3.50*
🍷 *Hot chocolate, £1.20*

ISLINGTON RESTAURANTS

Gallipoli Café

102 Upper Street, N1
(020) 7359 0630
⊖ Angel/Highbury and Islington

Generous portions of Turkish delights are what Gallipoli Café and its sister Bazaar down the street are all about. Pots and pans smash, people chat noisily as they share their plates of meze and no one seems to mind the general air of chaos. Frequently populated by hen and birthday parties, this teeny cave of fun is one of our faves on bustling Upper Street. There are loads of one-person dishes, but sharing's always more fun.

© *Mon–Thu, 12pm–11pm; Fri, 12pm–12am; Sat, 10am–12am; Sun, 10pm–10.30pm*

⊕ *Average dinner, £20 per person with wine*

FishWorks Seafood Café

134 Upper Street, N1
(020) 7354 1279
⊖ Highbury and Islington

So your parents are in town and you've not the faintest idea where to take them? If they like a bit of fish, then they'll absolutely love this place. From the homemade taramasalata to the grilled swordfish with Moroccan spices, everything about this relatively simple looking restaurant is fresh, clean and tastefully tasty. Eye up your dinner on the fish counter and then sit back with a crisp Chardonnay while it's cooked the way you want it. There's nothing fishy about this place.

© *Tue–Fri, 12pm–2.30pm & 6pm–10.15pm; Sat–Sun, 12pm–10.15pm*

⊕ *Salt-baked bream, £14.50*

Duke of Cambridge

30 St Peters Street, N1
(020) 7359 3066
⊖ Angel

It's big, busy and smells absolutely divine. It's one of those places you want to snuggle up in by candlelight when it's cold outside. Good beers and ciders on tap, plus we had one of the best Shiraz wines we've ever tasted in here, but it's hardly surprising – everything's organic, meaning super good for you, of course. Well, we like to tell ourselves that anyway. Can get a bit loud at weekends, but it's tucked away from the droves, so if you go early enough it shouldn't be a problem.

© *Mon–Sat, 12.30pm–3.30pm & 6.30pm–10.30pm; Sun, 12.30pm–3.30pm & 6.30pm–10pm*

⊕ *Rabbit and mash, £12*

Hamburger Union

341 Upper Street, N1
(020) 7359 4436
⊖ Angel

Cow lovers, look away now. There's only one reason God created Hamburger Union: to serve up piles of prime beef to hordes of slathering flesh-heads. Ok, so they also do something very tasty with grilled halloumi, but what they're best at is meat. Whether you like your burger with cheese, bacon, onions, salad, sauce, bleeding, single, double, for breakfast, lunch or dinner, you'll find it here. The only complaint we've got is the name; surely Hamburger Heaven would be a lot more appropriate.

© *Sun–Mon, 11.30am–9.30pm; Tue–Sat, 11.30am–10.30pm*

⊕ *Double cheeseburger, £7.45*

North

KING'S CROSS

6 St Chad's Place

6 St Chad's Place, WC1
(020) 7278 3355
⊖ King's Cross

Despite the drippy name, the bar itself is a refreshing change from the more old-skool drinking dens in the area. Housed in a former loco shed behind the Thameslink station, Chad's is airy and classy, playing host to locals in the know and the occasional bunch of Friday feeling city folk. Best of all, its hidden location makes it the perfect opportunity to show off your 'insider knowledge' (no, really, there's no need to thank us) of London.

Ⓒ *Mon–Fri, 8am–11pm*
Ⓝ *Deep fried whitebait, £3.50*
Ⓟ *£11*

The Big Chill House

257–259 Pentonville Road, N1
(020) 7427 2540
⊖ King's Cross

With its obvious passion for wide-ranging music, digital media and friendly staff, Big Chill House gives you more of a glow than if you mainlined Ready Brek. If you've been to the festival, prepare to get nostalgic; the myriad of fairytale rooms over three floors reflect classic Chill themes, including a cosy wooden Finlandia Cabin complete with transparent rocking chair, and a reflective lily pond table in the Enchanted Bar.

Ⓒ *Restaurant, Mon–Fri, 12pm–3pm; Bar food, Mon–Wed, 12pm–11pm; Thu–Sat, 12pm–6pm; Sun, 6pm–11pm; Sunday brunch, 12pm–6pm*
Ⓟ *£11*

Canal 125

125 Caledonian Road, N1
(020) 7837 1924
⊖ King's Cross

Itchy's endless quest for the perfect Sunday roast looked like it might be nearing its climax when someone told us that the roast beef in this place was half an inch thick and that the parsnips were honeyed. A large three level bar/restaurant within spitting distance of King's Cross, Canal 125 boasts comfy sofas and friendly staff with ace grub to boot. There are two rooms upstairs holding 70 and 140 people respectively, and the latter has its own outside dining area. And yes, the roast dinner is superb. Perhaps we can put our search on hold for a while.

Ⓒ *Mon–Sat, 12pm–12am; Sun, 12pm–10.30pm*
Ⓝ *Salmon fishcakes, £9.95*

BELSIZE PARK

The George

250 Haverstock Hill, NW3

(020) 7431 0889

⊖ Belsize Park/Chalk Farm

There really isn't anything particularly special about this pub, but we love its comfy, cosy charms. In the summer you can eat and drink outside on the sun-drenched terrace, and there's always a lively crowd. Occasional live music nights are fun if you're in the area, but we wouldn't travel here especially. If you're looking for a nice pub lunch after a leisurely stroll, or a quiet drink while you get your night off to a good start, The George is your man.

🕲 *Mon–Sun, 10am–11pm*

✪ *£11.15*

The Roebuck

15 Pond Street, NW3

(020) 7433 6871

⊖ Belsize Park

Have you recently awoken in the morning to think, 'God, I feel really old today'? Well, fear not granddad, this is the place you should head to if you're feeling more mature than Des O'Connor's stilton collection, as once inside you're free to peruse the papers, order a Guinness, talk about gardening and eat some lovely pie and mash. The music's low and pleasant and the crowd are, erm, how shall we put this... of a certain age. Grab yourself some talc, grey the hair up and take a pair of slippers to change into once you're there and you'll probably fit in.

🕲 *Mon–Sat, 12pm–11pm; Sun, 12pm–10.30pm*

✪ *£10*

Little Bay

228 Belsize Road, NW6

(020) 7372 4699

⊖ Kilburn Park

Kilburn ain't exactly where the action is in North London, (except for maybe sneaking in the back door of the Irish Centre for free and vomiting in the toilets – a fave Itchy pastime) but it's worth the trip for this place. Ask for a table upstairs, which resembles something between a wooden ship and a tree house. The wonderful food at unbelievably cheap prices means you can indulge in three courses for only £11.85 (£8.65 if you order before 7pm). A starter of marinated mussels for £3 has to be tasted to be believed. Ace.

🕲 *Mon–Sat, 12pm–12am; Sun, 12pm–11pm*

🕕 *Pork with pea and aubergine caviar, £4.75*

✪ *£9.95*

North

HAMPSTEAD

La Creperie de Hampstead
77 Hampstead High Street, NW3
(020) 7589 8947
⊖ Hampstead

Just down the hill from Hampstead station, this permanent takeaway stall serves up crepes as good, if not better, than anything you'd get in France. Amazingly, the ingredients for everything from cheese and ham to Belgian chocolate can be stored and cooked in this tiny trailer, and the results are mouthwatering. Eat them on a bench and watch Hampstead's high life. It's hugely popular at weekends, so expect to queue.

🕐 *Mon–Thu, 11.45am–11pm; Fri–Sun, 11.45am–11.30pm*

🍴 *Ham and cheese crepe, £5.95*

HIGHGATE

Boogaloo
312 Archway Road, N6
(020) 8340 2928
⊖ Highgate

We absolutely adore this place – it's one of those sacred spots where you can walk around and talk to anyone. The *GQ* award-winning jukebox is infamous – with every song approved by either a top musician, or having passed the ten year rule (no cheesy pop here unless it's pre-1997). You'll stay as long as it's open, you'll spend a lot behind the bar and you'll feel like shite the next day, but such is the beauty of the Boogaloo.

🕐 *Mon–Wed, 6pm–12am; Thu, 6pm–1am; Fri–Sat, 2pm–2am; Sun, 6pm–12am*

The Pineapple
51 Leverton Street, NW5
(020) 7284 4631
⊖ Kentish Town

It might be very much a local's pub, but that don't mean that there's something of the Royston Vasey about it. The difference between this little Kentish Town backstreet gem and most boozers is that you'll be treated like a local, even if you aren't. Squish up and make friends over a pint, or order some hearty British food and heckle people to play a tune on the old piano. Or turn up on a Monday and take part in the legendary pub quiz – one of the best in London. You don't get many pubs like this any more. Added bonus: we love the old coal fire. Mmmm, cosy.

🕐 *Mon–Sat, 12pm–11.30pm; Sun, 12pm–10.30pm*

Derelict London

YOU MIGHT THINK THAT THERE'S NEW STUFF OPENING ALL THE TIME IN LONDON, BUT IT'S EASY TO FORGET THE STUFF THAT CLOSES DOWN. HERE'S ITCHY'S SELECT FEW LOST LONDON TREASURES

1 **The London Necropolis Railway Station** (121 Westminster Bridge Road, SE1). This railway line was built specifically for the purpose of transporting the dead and their mourners to the Brookwood Cemetery. Opened in 1854, the station was closed in 1941 when it was struck by bombs. The remains of the building still stand on Westminster Bridge Road.

2 **Down Street Tube Station**, (Down Street, W1). Opened in 1907, it was closed in 1932 along with a slew of less busy stations. Its main claim to fame is its use in 1939 as a bunker for Churchill and his cabinet before the Cabinet War Rooms were built. Oh, and it's famous – you can spot it in the film *Creep*, and speculation abounds about it being the disused station featured in *Die Another Day*.

3 Not all derelict places tell entertaining stories. In 2000, Newham Council granted permission to build flats on **Woodgrange Park Cemetery** in Manor Park (Newham, E12), which resulted in human remains being hauled over by mechanical diggers before families had a chance to move them and the headstones being donated to make a graveyard in *Emmerdale*.

4 **The Roundhouse** (Chalk Farm Road, NW1) is a real treasure regained. Transformed from an engine shed into an important music venue in the 60s and 70s (Bowie, Hendrix and The Doors played here), The Roundhouse closed in 1983 and stood empty 'til June 2006 when it was reopened as a theatre and, fingers crossed, will remain open for some time to come.

WHO
WHAT
WHERE
WHEN
IS X?

LUXARDO X TEAM COMING
TO HOT NIGHTSPOTS NEAR YOU!

GAMES, GIVEAWAYS,
COMPETITIONS, PRIZES

WWW.LUXARDOXTEAM.CO.UK FOR
MORE ABOUT WHO, WHAT, WHERE & WHEN X IS

LUXARDO
1 8 2 1
SAMBUCA
THE MARK OF SUPERIORITY

East

East

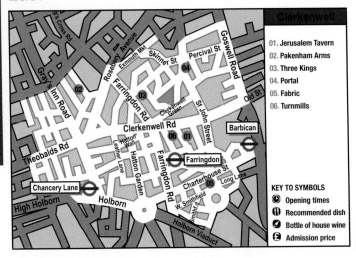

Clerkenwell

01. Jerusalem Tavern
02. Pakenham Arms
03. Three Kings
04. Portal
05. Fabric
06. Turnmills

KEY TO SYMBOLS

🕐 Opening times
🍴 Recommended dish
🍷 Bottle of house wine
💷 Admission price

CLERKENWELL PUBS

Jerusalem Tavern

55 Britton Street, EC1
(020) 7490 4281
⊖ Farringdon

Tucked away in genteel Clerkenwell, the Jerusalem Tavern is a fine venue to stage a crusade of your own. In this case the prize is not the Ark of the Covenant, but rather those barrels up behind the bar, containing a mysterious elixir known as real ale. Far from the usual nasty bleachy smoothflow, this stuff is a drink worthy of heroes. The interior looks like it's straight out of a mediaeval alehouse too, so find yourself a dark corner and strike out for fame, fortune and a liver-twisting hangover.

🕐 *Mon–Fri, 11am–11pm*

Pakenham Arms

1 Pakenham Street, WC1
(020) 7837 6933
⊖ Farringdon/Russell Square

If Postman Pat really did run over his cat, it was probably because he'd had a couple too many down the Pakenham after hours, then tried to bust bunny-hops in his Pat wagon. Catering almost exclusively to the employees of Mount Pleasant sorting depot across the road, the unsociable hours of postie work mean that this beauty is usually open 'til one. The regulars are much friendlier than you'd expect, the beer is good and best of all there's a dartboard. Mrs Pat might be a Pakenham widow, but at least she's got Jess for company. Oh, wait…

🕐 *Mon–Sat, 9am–1am; Sun, 9am–10.30pm*

Three Kings Of Clerkenwell

7 Clerkenwell Close, EC1

(020) 7253 0483

⊖ Farringdon/Chancery Lane

The Old Speckled Hen here is the most famous thing on wings since Kes, and a damn sight better at quenching a thirst to boot. The décor may scream 90s naffness, but the Three Kings is nevertheless an Itchy favourite for mooching around on a quiet afternoon or evening when you all you want to do is listen to a decent jukebox with only a stuffed rhino head for company (it's not real, by the way). If you like your Corrie then you might well be in for a treat, as ex-cast member Spider apparently pulls the odd pint here.

🕒 Mon–Fri, 12pm–11pm; Sat, 7pm–11pm; Food, Mon–Fri, 12pm–4pm

CLERKENWELL CLUBS

Fabric

77a Charterhouse Street, EC1

(020) 7336 8898

⊖ Farringdon

Fabric proves that a big London club can succeed without selling out to the evils of big-name DJs playing incessant kiddie trance. Instead, the club that was once a meat warehouse provides an underground electro/breaks/drum 'n' bass party in the form of Fabriclive on a Friday, and on Saturdays you get the Fabric house and techno session. Yes, it's crowded beyond belief, but it's also where you'll hear the best DJs in the world every weekend. Now isn't that worth a trampled toe?

🎟 Fri, 9.30pm–5am, £12; Sat, 10pm–7am, £15

CLERKENWELL RESTAURANTS

Portal

88 St John Street, EC1

(020) 253 6950

⊖ Farringdon/Barbican

First port of call for laid-back luxury and non-threatening poshness. Request a table in the conservatory, and listen to the waiters; these guys have encyclopaedic knowledge of what they serve. As for the vino… when even the olive oil has a vintage, you know the wine ain't gonna be shoddy. If port is more than a coal-tinged tipple left out for Santa once a year for you, then all your Christmases just came at once.

🕒 Mon–Sat, 12pm–3pm & 6pm–10.15pm

🍴 Braised Bisaro wild boar, £18

Turnmills

63b Clerkenwell Road, EC1

(020) 7250 3409

⊖ Farringdon

Turnmills (or 'Gurnpills' as some wags have been known to call it) is a club of two personalities. On Fridays, it's all about The Gallery, the trance and techno night that sees Judge Jules and friends banging out the big tunes like there's no tomorrow, but on Saturdays things get a lot more varied – thankfully. With NYE night Together going monthly (and attracting the likes of Fischerspooner and Justice as guests and Justin Robertson as a resident) and other Saturdays like Smartie Partie and Kinky Malinki, fans of funky house and electro are well catered for by this clubland stalwart.

🎟 Fri, 10.30pm–7am, £12; Sat, 10pm–6am, £15

East

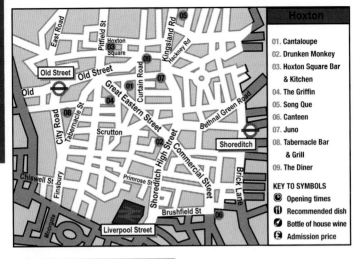

Hoxton

01. Cantaloupe
02. Drunken Monkey
03. Hoxton Square Bar & Kitchen
04. The Griffin
05. Song Que
06. Canteen
07. Juno
08. Tabernacle Bar & Grill
09. The Diner

KEY TO SYMBOLS
- © Opening times
- 🍴 Recommended dish
- 🍷 Bottle of house wine
- 💷 Admission price

HOXTON BARS

Cantaloupe
35–42 Charlotte Road, EC2
(020) 7729 5566
⊖ Shoreditch

The relaxed, funky vibe at this well-established bar makes it a must to visit if you're ever trawling the Old Street area of a night. Cantaloupe attracts early evening post-work drinkers, who later mix with, and are then replaced by the hip (though not painfully so) locals. There's a good selection of drinks (including pints on tap) and the food's undoubtedly more interesting than your average burger and chips.

© *Mon–Fri, 11am–12am; Sat, 12pm–12am; Sun, 12pm–11.30pm; Food, Mon–Fri, 12pm–3pm & 6pm–11pm; Sat, 7pm–11pm*

Drunken Monkey
222 Shoreditch High Street, E1
(020) 7392 9606
⊖ Shoreditch

Get to the Drunken Monkey at 4.55pm if you want a table – it fills up quickly. The crowd is a mix of city types coming from one direction and dope young things gravitating from the other, which makes for a bustling atmosphere with regular DJ spots. There's a great range of decently-priced cocktails, and expect dim sum if you're after food – it's pleasantly different and soaks up the booze well. This is a good new venue, which is easy to miss with its unremarkable façade, perhaps a throwback from its earlier incarnation as a lap-dancing bar.

© *Mon–Fri, 12pm–12.30am; Sat, 6pm–12.30am; Sun, 12pm–11.30pm*

Hoxton Square Bar and Kitchen

2–4 Hoxton Square, N1

(020) 7613 0709

⊖ Old Street/Shoreditch

A much-loved East London haunt, this great bar epitomises Hoxton-chic and serves up some decent food into the bargain. It's pretty laid back and the rag tag collection of sofas, chairs and stools mean you can lounge with a Sunday afternoon cider or sit around with mates on a night out. The back room also stages regular gigs but check before you go as the line-up and timings change on a weekly basis.

🕔 *Mon–Thu & Sun, 11am–1am; Fri–Sat, 11am–1am; Food, Mon–Sun, 12pm–10pm*

🍴 *Flaming 8 Burger, £9.50*

🟡 *£12*

The Strongrooms

120 Curtain Road, EC2

(020) 7426 5100

⊖ Old Street

Tucked away down a very nice little mews, this compact but cosy bar serves up a few interesting beers and some propah Lahndan pie and mash dishes. It's easy to spend a whole day here doing nothing much at all, so if you've recently received a massive redundancy package or you've just inherited millions from a great aunt you never knew existed, this is the place to fritter it away. Those of us not blessed with an abundance of time or money will have to make do with midweek drinks in relaxing surroundings or toe-tapping at one of the regular DJ nights.

🕔 *Mon–Thu, 12pm–11pm; Fri–Sat, 12pm–2am*

Juno

134–135 Shoreditch High Street, E1

(020) 7729 2660

⊖ Old Street/Shoreditch

Pretty small and innocent-looking from the outside, but enter and you'll be lucky to escape before the last tube – Juno sucks you in and then some, even to the point where Itchy once lost some shoes here. If you happen to see a pair of white Converse in the corner please donate the rotten things to the nearest rubbish tip. It's open 'til late, and the downstairs has some great little crannies as well as the occasional opportunity for a boogie. A bit more friendly than your average Old Street bar and home to some penny-sappingly addictive retro arcade games.

🕔 *Times vary*

Tabernacle Bar & Grill

55–61 Tabernacle Street, EC2

(020) 7253 5555

⊖ Old Street

Itchy doesn't understand why this funky bar isn't full every night of the week. Perhaps it's because the venue's just off the beaten track, in the dark back streets connecting Old Street and City Road. The restaurant service can be slow, yet the waiters are honest in their recommendations, and the grub is as nice as pie. This is a hidden diamond, first uncovered when Shoreditch was 'up and coming' but seemingly forgotten since, as attentions have turned to the next 'place to be'.

🕔 *Restaurant, Mon–Fri, 12pm–3pm & 6pm–12am; bar, Mon–Wed, 8.30am–12am; Thu–Sat, 8.30am–2am*

East

HOXTON PUBS

The Griffin

93 Leonard Street, EC2

(020) 7739 6719

⚪ Old Street

It might look like the Blitz has just finished and the only thing left standing amongst the deserted warehouses was this old boozer. Thank God it was this one, and not any of the other swanky, wanky bars round here. This is a proper pub, with beer, locals, a jukebox and a bit of a car park where they put out chairs in the summer. You get the odd cool kid stopping by, but they behave themselves and enjoy a night of old–fashioned drinking like everyone else. Now that's what we call London pride.

◎ *Mon–Sat, 11am–11pm; Sun, 12pm–10.30pm*

HOXTON CLUBS

Browns

1 Hackney Road, E2

(020) 7739 3565

⚪ Old Street/Shoreditch

If you thought that sweaty, flea-pit strip joints were solely the domain of bad American movies aimed at adolescents then you haven't been to Browns. Naked flesh in the form of women's bits and men's tongues hanging out is on offer nightly, and a lady, usually called Tatyana or Crystal, will come round and demand a couple of quid off you every now and then for the pleasure. This one's strictly for stag parties, cheering up a recently dumped mate or the very, very drunk.

◎ *Times vary*

William IV

7 Shepherdess Walk, N1

(020) 3119 3011

⚪ Old Street

A little Hoxton gastropub that looks like it's been converted directly from the common room of an Edwardian boarding school, complete with black and white pictures of the 1st XI and the rowing team lining the stairs, as well as some very funny looking choristers. On the first floor there's a geography-themed room, and a little room decked up as the headmaster's study. The food's amazing – the Eton mess alone is like eating heaven or God, or something equally divine.

◎ *Mon–Wed, 12pm–11pm; Thu–Sat, 12pm–12am; Sun, 12pm–10.30pm*

Ⓟ *Eton mess, £4.50*

HOXTON CAFÉS

Song Que

134 Kingsland Road, E2

(020) 7613 3222

⊖ Old Street/Shoreditch

Vietnamese food is an Itchy fave, and this decent-sized café serves up some of the best you'll find west of Hanoi. It can be busy, but if you find a decent table-space a massive array of noodle dishes and dozens of side dishes await your eager taste buds. The best are undoubtedly the spring rolls and crispy shredded duck – both will leave you desperate to make the slightly lengthy trek from the tube to Song Que again and again.

Ⓒ *Mon–Sat, 5.30pm–11pm; Sun, 12pm–11pm*

Ⓘ *Beef noodle soup, £5.25*

The Diner

128 Curtain Road, EC2

(020) 7729 4452

⊖ Old Street

This late-night delight for the Sho'ditch party massive is, as you might imagine, American. The Diner offers burgers, fries 'n' shakes, and the sort of brekkies that have been obesifying our cousins across the pond for years. Great for a hangover, whether it's the 'pre-emptive strike before bedtime' or the languid 'morning-after-the-night-before'. Blueberry pancakes, eggs over-easy, streaky bacon, wheat toast AND syrup? Yeah, homes. Fill your boots. And try the cawfee.

Ⓒ *Mon–Sun, 8am–11.20pm*

Ⓘ *Bacon cheeseburger, £6.20*

Ⓐ *£13–£14*

HOXTON RESTAURANTS

Canteen

Spitalfields Market, 2 Crispin Place, E1

(08456) 861 122

⊖ Liverpool Street/Aldgate East

Canteen lies in the middle of newly-refurbished Spitalfields Market and offers modern British cuisine in a restaurant that looks like a Danish motorway service station. The food's great – they do lots of pies, kippers, roasts, and treacle tarts, etc – and the staff are perky. We'd recommend going for brunch after you've bought your knick-knacks and olive bread nearby. Best book first though. This place is usually chocka.

Ⓒ *Mon–Fri, 8am–11pm; Sat–Sun, 9am–11pm*

Ⓘ *Pork belly with apples, £10*

Ⓐ *£12*

Shish

313–319 Old Street, EC1

(020) 7749 0990

⊖ Old Street

Just as café owners up and down the country long ago realised the appeal of chips and put them with everything on their menus, so the brains behind Shish have understood that there's no better way to cook something than to stick it on a skewer and roast it to perfection. Taking ingredients from the length of the Silk Road (Italy to Japan for anyone who used to spend geography lessons catching up on sleep), this is pan-world food on a stick.

Ⓒ *Mon–Fri, 11am–12am; Sat, 10.30am–12am; Sun, 10.30am–11pm*

Ⓘ *Afghan chicken, £8.25*

Ⓐ *£11.95*

East

BRICK LANE/WHITECHAPEL

93 Feet East

Truman Brewery, 150 Brick Lane, E1

(020) 7247 3293

⊖ Shoreditch/Liverpool Street

An old Itchy favourite for late night boozing and grooving in Brick Lane, 93 Feet East is home to some excellent electro and indie mash-ups. The sprawling courtyard is popular in the summer – especially as they do the odd bit of burger grilling when it's warm enough – and the inside is a mixture of gig venue and a more sociable bar area. Shoreditch attitudes aside, it's a nice place to end up on a Friday night, and the curry emporium of Brick Lane is on your doorstep for after-hours nosh.

🕒 *Times and prices vary*

New Tayyabs

83–89 Fieldgate Street, E1

(020) 72476400

⊖ Whitechapel

Brick Lane missions are a bit hit and miss; sometimes they can be legendary, but very often they can be a tad disappointing, even if they are cheaper than our puns. So you might do well to wander on down to the boho surroundings of Whitechapel and try the rather fragrant Tayyabs. It may sound like a Welsh word for loutish children but the food is proper Punjabi and utterly divine. Daily specials offer a cornucopia of spicy dishes – Sunday's tinda masala being particularly worth leaving the house for. Curry with class.

🕒 *Mon–Sun, 5pm–11.30pm*

🍴 *Lamb curry, £5.20*

Lahore Kebab House

2 Umberston Street, E1

(020) 7488 2551

⊖ Algate East/Whitechapel/Shadwell DLR

Forget Brick Lane. This legendary restaurant has been packing 'em in and knocking 'em out for over 20 years now. So the service isn't arse-kissy, the décor is circa 1983 and there's a photo of the owner with his pet lion next to the till, but hey. The food is consistently top-drawer and will cost you slightly more than a pack of fags. The menu isn't extensive, but that's a good thing if your attention span is short and your belly is empty. Bring your own booze and order the lamb karahi.

🕒 *Mon–Sun, 5pm–1.30am*

🍴 *Lamb karahi, £4.95*

🍷 *BYO*

Pride of Spitalfields

3 Heneage Street, E1

(020) 7247 8933

⊖ Shoreditch/Aldgate East

Unlike many pub names this one actually describes the boozer behind the sign to a tee; it really is one of the nicest old-fashioned public houses in the historic Spitalfields area and Itchy's rather fond of it. Compared to your average Wethbarsluglodge Arms, it's a gem, with relatively petite, but elegantly aged proportions and a fine selection of ales befitting a pub of the Pride's repute. A great antidote to some of the more pretentious bars and pubs nearby.

🕒 *Mon–Sat, 11am–11pm; Sun, 12pm–10.30pm; Food, Mon–Fri, 12pm–2.30pm; Sun, 1pm–5pm*

The Vibe Bar

Old Truman Brewery, 91 Brick Lane, E1

(020) 7247 3479

⊖ Shoreditch/Liverpool Street

A stalwart among East London hang-outs, and home to probably the biggest alfresco boozing area in these trendy parts. Like some sort of newly-discovered party island, Vibe boasts several distinct habitats in which to while away a few hours – they have relaxing sofas, a groovy little dance floor and, of course, the massive outdoor section complete with more benches and tables than a French motorway service station. An ideal hunting ground for thrill-seekers.

🕒 *Mon–Thu & Sun, 12pm–11.30pm; Fri–Sat, 12pm–1am*

💰 *Prices vary*

The Ten Bells

84 Commercial Street, E1

(020) 7366 1721

⊖ Liverpool Street/Shoreditch

A must-drink-in pub if you're interested in some of London's darker historical characters. This is the place where Jack The Ripper's victims drank their last drink before being knifed in the nearby streets, so if you like serial killers (and who doesn't?) then The Ten Bells is virtually a theme park with a drinking licence. It is pretty small (folk were either shorter or so drunk they could only crawl in and out when it was first opened in 1753) and the selection of beers is limited, but it's cosy and interesting if you like your pubs with a bit of history.

🕒 *Mon–Wed & Sun, 11am–12am; Thu–Sat, 11am–1am*

East

BETHNAL GREEN

The Approach Tavern

47 Approach Road, E2

(020) 8980 2321

⊖ Bethnal Green/Cambridge Heath (BR)

A cracking East London boozer with pleasant urban surroundings and staff, a beer garden, a fine selection of pub food and an art gallery upstairs. The Approach fits very much into the mould of the trendy Hoxton hangout but don't let that put you off – it's popular for good reason and you'll often get a seat due to its ample size. A cut above the competition in E2.

◉ Mon–Thu & Sun, 12pm–11pm; Fri–Sat, 12pm–1am; Food, Mon–Fri, 12pm–2.30pm & 6pm–9.30pm; Sat, 12pm–9.30pm; Sun, 12pm–5pm

Bethnal Green Working Men's Club

44–46 Pollard Row, E2

(020) 7739 7170

⊖ Bethnal Green

While not quite as famous as the one in Manchester where that Smiths photo was taken, London's coolest WMC is a multi-faceted venue where you can watch short films, dance the night away, see a play or be slightly scared by some sleazy cabaret. They also have a unique take on the Sunday-in-the-pub session in Take A Load Off Fanny (yes, it is 'off' not 'of'), spent lounging around with board games, vitamin-packed juices and interesting film ditties running on a projector. Effortless East London chic and always entertaining.

◉ Times and prices vary

Décor blimey

When it comes to things weird and wonderful, London's got 'em in bucket-loads. But if it's some freaky eye-candy to intrigue you while you down your G&Ts you're after, there are plenty of places to satisfy. We like **Loungelover** (1 Whitby Street, E2, 020 7012 1234) – with its flaming torches and antique décor it's a surrealist's wet dream. Not one for the easily scared is **Waxy's Little Sister** (20 Wardour Street, W1, 020 7287 8987) in Soho. Upstairs is like the inside of a smurf house – you know, a mushroom. Yellow walls, massive sofas and a balcony overlooking the door mean the day-trippers, (or just the trippers) are amused for hours. Oh and don't take your porridge into **The Endurance** (90 Berwick Street, W1, 020 7437 2944). The stuffed grizzly bear will eye it up all night, until someone throws their jacket over its head.

Café Booze

87 Lauriston Road, E9

(020) 8985 8941

⊖ London Fields (BR)/Homerton (BR)

Not greatly advertised, but a definite fave for the Sunday strollers, this is the quintessential English café, complete with a grumpy waitress and screaming kid (belonging to said grumpy waitress). But we are there because they serve the best greasy fry up we've ever found inside the M25, and believe us, we've had a few. Its cute chequered tablecloths and massive mugs of steaming tea, plus sought-after garden space in the summer make the perfect stop for curing your aching body of the night before.

🕲 *Mon–Sun, 9am–5.30pm*

🍴 *Full English breakfast, £5.50*

The Camel

227 Globe Road, E2

(020) 8983 9888

⊖ Bethnal Green/Stepney Green

Complete with a piano that cost the owners five quid on eBay, this side street Bethnal Green pub is a classic, and a firm fave with the locals who all signed a petition when they threatened to turn it into a block of flats. Retro lighting and funky wallpaper attract the Shoreditch wanderers in search of perhaps the best pie and mash in town, all handmade with gourmet fillings, such as Jerusalem artichoke and Stilton, or chicken Madras. It's no smoking though, so puff outside while you can.

🕲 *Mon–Sat, 12pm–11pm; Sun, 12pm–10.30pm*

🍴 *Pie and mash, £7.95*

💲 *£12*

Café Isha

115a Roman Road, E2

(020) 8980 4555

⊖ Mile End/Bow Road

When it first opened, this little treasure had no licence and half the fun of coming was bringing your own liquor and snuggling up for some quiet boozing in the Aladdin's cave they call the Sultan's Lounge. Now that they serve alcohol, the local yobs have found it, and the portions of (very good) Lebanese food have gotten considerably smaller. Hunger and thugs aside, it's still a decent place to take a few mates and get stuck into some shish. Try the apple, and chill out.

🕲 *Mon–Sun, 11am–11pm*

🍴 *Lamb with lentils, ginger and garlic, £5.95*

Mercado

26–30 Stoke Newington Church Street, N16

(020) 7923 0555

⊖ Angel, then 73 bus

You couldn't get more colour in a place if you stuffed it with folded rainbows. Bedazzling with fairy lights, painted tyres and originality, Mercado grub is miles away from typical conveyor belt Tex-Mex; lamb baked in banana leaves and steamed cactus will raise your eyebrows in surprise, then sipping tequilas and Tamazula Tabasco will blow them clean off. Everything Mexican comes straight from there, everything else is sourced locally, and every face sports a whopping smile. Colour us very happy indeed.

🕲 *Mon–Wed, 6pm–11pm; Thu–Fri, 12pm–3pm & 6pm–11pm; Sat–Sun, 11am–11pm*

🍴 *Chicken tortilla with chocolate mole, £9.50*

East

Frocks

95 Lauriston Road, E9

(020) 8986 3161

⊖ London Fields (BR)/Homerton (BR)

Nothing to do with dresses, apart from the fact that you'll go up a size once you've been. 'A gourmet who thinks of calories is like a tart who looks at her watch', reads one of the quotes on the wall of this snug, two-floor diamond; you won't be looking at your timepiece, but you will be looking at your tart (or whatever else you've ordered from the deluxe European menu) and wondering if it's made from pastry or edible magic.

🅒 *Mon–Fri, 6.30pm–10.30pm; Sat, 11am–3pm & 6.30pm–10.30pm; Sun, 12pm–9pm*

🅜 *Mon–Wed, 2 starters, 2 mains and a bottle of wine, £40*

🅞 *£11.75*

LMNT

316 Queensbridge Road, E8

(020) 7249 6727

⊖ London Fields (BR)

Itchy loves a bit of sauce over dinner, but you may get more than just hollandaise on your fishcakes at the richly decorated LMNT if you wander into the bathrooms – the tile paintings inside would make Hugh Hefner blush. But don't come here just for the smutty décor, as their lunch and dinner menus offer some of the best value European fare in East London in very extravagant surroundings. Opera à la Carte on Sunday is a touch of highbrow, on-the-cheap brilliance.

🅒 *Times vary*

🅜 *Confit of lamb shoulder, £8.95*

🅞 *£10.95*

Games for a laugh

Balls Pond Road in Dalston takes its name from a Mr Ball, who had a duck pond outside his pub, hundreds of years ago. For a fee, drunken punters could shoot the poor blighters for fun. Now the most you can do is shoot pinball at **The Royal George** (Goslett Yard, WC2, 020 7734 8837) off Charing Cross Road. The **Old Coffee House** (49 Beak Street, W1, 020 7437 2197) in Soho is great for darts, and further North **The Freemason's Arms** (32 Downshire Hill, NW3, 020 7433 6811) in Hampstead contains one of two remaining London pub skittle alleys. Out West, table football fans won't be disappointed with **The Three Kings** in Bayswater (171–173 North End Road, W14, 020 7603 6071) – their mini pitches kept Itchy happy for hours. Duck-hunters will have to make do with a trip to their local Chinese.

The Palm Tree

Haverfield Road, E3

(020) 8980 2918

⊖ Mile End

This is how all proper English pubs should be – dark, cosy and full of really old people who look like they started their pint before the war and never really left. It's true that this stand-alone number, hidden by bushes and aptly, a few palm trees, was the only thing in the vicinity not destroyed in the air raids. Let's all be thankful. This dismal area needs its charming live performers every Friday, Saturday and Sunday, when oldies and youngsters dance around the piano together.

☺ *Mon–Thu, 12pm–12am; Fri–Sat, 12pm–2am; Sun, 12pm–1am*

Winkles

238 Roman Road, E2

(020) 8880 7450

⊖ Mile End/Bow Road

Oysters, langoustine, clams, mussels, prawns. It's like the Little Mermaid's birthday party in this weirdly placed restaurant. They say the best places are the hardest to find and they're not wrong. Peer through the fish–netted windows and you'll find couples spooning tasty broths and making eyes over candlelit glasses of wine. People seem to be travelling from miles to eat in an area with nothing more around it than a few flats and a shut–up pub, so they must be doing something right.

☺ *Tue–Sat, 12pm–10.30pm; Sun, 12pm–9pm*

⊕ *Set dinner, £24.50*

Stingray Globe Café

109 Columbia Road, E2

(020) 7613 114

⊖ Old Street/Shoreditch

Top quality Italian food at reasonable prices doesn't exactly grow on trees east of Soho, but if you find yourself in E2 you'll be neither disappointed, nor on the phone to your bank manager after a blow-out at the Stingray. While they specialise in delicious rustic pizzas, they also serve the usual array of antipasti and starters at similarly wallet-friendly prices. It's not big and it can get busy, but the nearby Sunday flower market is worth a visit after lunch and a portion of their yummy tiramisu.

☺ *Mon–Sun, 11am–11pm*

⊕ *Mexicana pizza, £5.95*

❷ *£9.50*

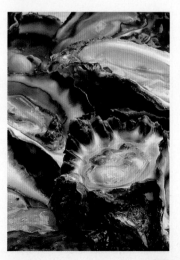

East

CITY

The Dickens Inn

St Katherine's Dock, Tower Bridge, E1
(020) 7488 2208
⊖ Tower Hill

1976 – Brazil get Ronaldo, we get The Dickens Inn – did we get a raw deal? Itchy doesn't think so. The Dickens hosts a passable pub area on the ground floor but the real draw are the dustbin lid-sized pizzas they serve on the top floor. This is a real summer destination, with hanging baskets and gorgeous views across the marina. Get a seat on the balcony so you can soak up the rays and drool at the beautiful young things sunbathing on the nearby yachts while you stuff your face.

Ⓒ Mon–Sun, 12pm–10pm

The Cuban

1 Ropemaker Street, EC2
(020) 7488 2208
⊖ Moorgate

That hottie from accounts is going to need something a little classy. A cocktail or two perhaps? Yeah, that'll be just the thing. So we go to our favourite castropub. It's called The Cuban. A mojito or three ought to tip the scales our way for sure. So far so good. There's laughter in all the right places, and we're even getting the odd little coy smile. Could this be the night it finally happens? We order a bite. It takes a while. Then longer. It comes. Cold. The waitress is nowhere to be seen. We leave. In two cabs. Close, but no cigar.

Ⓒ Mon–Fri, 8am–1am
Ⓝ Tapas, from £4

Stay regular

Illustration by Joly Braime

AIN'T NOTHIN' QUITE LIKE STEPPING INTO A BAR AND BEING GREETED AS ONE OF THEIR OWN. HERE'S ITCHY'S GUIDE TO BECOMING AS REGULAR AS CLOCKWORK SOMEWHERE NEW

1 **Learn the name of the publican's partner/pet/mum –** Take a couple of mates and stand at the bar within earshot of the publican and engage in the 'what would your porn name be?' game (combine your pet's name with your mum's maiden name). After a while, get the publican to join in, and make up some new variants designed to extract info about the names of spouses, dad, etc. Next time you walk in, you'll be able to greet them with a friendly, 'Alright Dave, how's Sandra doing?'

2 **Have your own pint mug –** Take a vessel and ask them to keep it behind the bar for you. Then whenever you walk in, you can sup your beverage in style. You may want to save this for the second visit.

3 **Know the pool rules –** If they've already got a set of rules in place, learn what they are, loiter near the table and make sure you pounce upon any infraction to loudly proclaim 'That's not how we do things in here'. If there are no house rules, even better – make some up, don't tell anyone what they are, and then soon everyone'll need to ask you before playing.

4 **Start a cribbage team –** Unless the pub in question's populated by incontinent octogenarians, there's no chance that they'll have one. Get a 'Captain' T-shirt, and swan round asking randoms if they're ready for the big match. They'll have no idea what you're talking about, allowing you to explain your importance to the pub community.

5 **Take a dog –** Everyone loves a dog. Well, except asthmatics. But who cares about them? Those guys are already having enough of a wheeze.

South

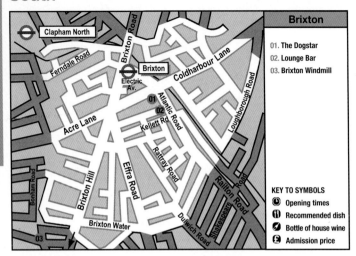

Brixton

01. The Dogstar
02. Lounge Bar
03. Brixton Windmill

KEY TO SYMBOLS

🕐 Opening times
🍴 Recommended dish
🍷 Bottle of house wine
🎫 Admission price

BRIXTON BARS

The Dogstar

389 Coldharbour Lane, SW9

(020) 7733 7515

⊖ Brixton

Situated on the corner of the infamous/ famous (delete as applicable depending on who you've been talking to) Coldhabour Lane, The Dogstar is a Brixton institution, and rightly so. It has a dark, classy feel, which somehow gives it a definite air of cool without being pretentious and, surprisingly enough, it serves some very palatable Tex-Mex nosh which is ideal for sharing over a few drinks.

🕐 *Club, Sun–Thu, 9pm–2am; Fri–Sat, 9pm–4am; bar, Mon–Thu, 4pm–2am; Fri–Sat & Sun, 12pm–4am*

Lounge Bar

88 Atlantic Road, SW9

(020) 7733 5229

⊖ Brixton

This little gem is highly reminiscent of an Old Street boho-bar with its low tables and quirky décor. It's right on one of the main market streets in Brixton, which means that on your way there you'll more than likely come across some pretty bizarre looking (and smelling) produce that would be a lot more recognisable if it still had legs or a tail. The walk there's not for the squeamish, so the calm atmosphere and wide selection of beers and snacks inside Lounge Bar are a welcome diversion from the carnage outside.

🕐 *Mon–Wed, 11am–11pm; Thu–Sat, 11am–12am; Sun, 11am–5.30pm*

BRIXTON PUBS

BarBar Black Sheep

60 Camberwell New Road, SE5

(020) 7735 9990

⊖ Oval

Itchy first discovered this place back when the rugby was on and hordes of indomitable Aussies packed it to the brim for beer at 8.30 in the morning. That was a few years ago, but we still head here over any other pub in London when there's a game on, and it's also a fine place for a quiet pint with some top gastro grub. It's not full of the morons who seem to enjoy smashing the windows on the same street, thank God. We love the free newspaper offerings on Sundays, too.

© Mon–Sun, 11am–11pm

BRIXTON CLUBS

Brixton Windmill

22 Blenheim Gardens, SW2

(020) 8671 0700

⊖ Brixton

Approach the much–loved Windmill without having been there before and you'll wonder why a youth club has an alcohol licence. Step inside and you'll find a cracking little indie club devoted to all things musical. It doesn't have an ounce of pretension and they serve snakebite and black – it's the perfect place to let your hair down while watching a band or two. It's a fair walk from the tube, so check out which buses you can hop on.

© Times and prices
depending on event

South London Pacific

340 Kennington Road, SE11

(020) 7820 9189

⊖ Kennington

Wander towards South Pacific, through the streets of Kennington, and the last thing you'll be expecting is a Hawaiian–themed club/bar boasting some of the naffest décor Itchy's seen since Graham Norton had to redecorate his bedroom in favour of something more subtle. Having said that, this place is a whole lot of fun and you can happily spend hours in South London Pacific sipping summery beers and dancing the hula. Dust off your flowery shirt and get a couple of lanky blokes with a broom handle to set up a limbo competition – aloha!

© Times and prices vary

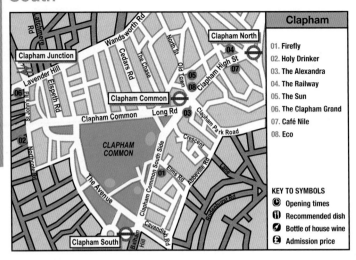

Clapham

01. Firefly
02. Holy Drinker
03. The Alexandra
04. The Railway
05. The Sun
06. The Clapham Grand
07. Café Nile
08. Eco

KEY TO SYMBOLS

- Opening times
- Recommended dish
- Bottle of house wine
- Admission price

CLAPHAM BARS

Bierodrome

44–48 Clapham High Street, SW4

(020) 7720 1118

⊖ Clapham North

This is clever – combine the rather obvious pairing of beer and an aerodrome and what do you have? The Bierodrome, obviously. The person who first combined serving a wide range of delicious foreign beers in a space shaped like a WWII aerodrome (sharply curved roof, etc) deserves a pat on the back, but we hear he's gone into bigger and better things. All we're saying is look out for a Vodkaravan on a high street near you at some point in 2007.

Sun–Thu, 12pm–12am;
Fri–Sat, 12pm–2am

The Fine Line

182 Clapham High Street, SW4

(020) 7622 4436

⊖ Clapham Common

Although part of a chain, this tasteful bar is a relaxing alternative to some of the more in–your–face drinking holes nearby. It's a great place for a casual drink or a Sunday afternoon blow out on one of their fine roast lunches. Everyone knows that the best antidote to a weekend (and possibly a week) of excess is to put yourself into a food coma with a big plate of meat and gravy, and if you're lucky you may even get yourself serenaded by a David Gray wannabe on one of the bi–monthly Sunday afternoon gigs.

Mon–Thu & Sun, 11am–11pm;
Fri–Sat, 11am–1am

Firefly

69 Clapham Common South Side, SW4

(020) 8673 9162

⊖ Clapham South

Although this modern bar is a little bit off the beaten track, it's worth seeking out whatever the weather. You can sit out on the sunny benches on the days when the weather is vaguely warm and the drizzle stops for a few minutes, or retreat to the comfy sofas and stools inside for the other 363 days of the year. It's also on the pleasanter side of quiet because of the location and they serve really decent food, making the Firefly a perfect destination for lunch and drinks or a relaxing weekday evening out.

🍷 *Mon–Thu, 5pm–12am; Fri, 5pm–1am; Sat, 12pm–1am; Sun, 12pm–12am*

Holy Drinker

59 Northcote Road, SW11

(020) 7801 0544

⊖ Clapham South/Clapham Common

Situated on the Junction's relatively soulless Northcote Road, this saintly little bolthole is a cut above the nearby competition and serves a lovely selection of beers and spirits. They boast a well thought out music policy, and their venue name is no idle boast either. After all, what could be more holy than spending a Sunday in The Drinker at 'the morning after', their weekly laid-back day of soothing music, healthy fruit juices and log fires. A bit of that and you'll be ready to hit the beers again by the afternoon.

🍷 *Mon–Fri & Sun, 'til 11pm; Sat, 'til 12am*

CLAPHAM PUBS

The Alexandra

14 Clapham Common South Side, SW4

(020) 7627 5102

⊖ Clapham Common

A firm Itchy favourite, this palatial two-levelled pub is situated right beside Clapham Common in a pleasant high street location. You can drink 'til you fall off your stool in the first floor pub or gaze into the eyes of a gorgeous young lady in the more sophisticated upstairs bar. Well, until the gorgeous young lady gets the bouncer to throw you out for constantly staring at her anyway. The Alex is also a good place to watch sport and they serve a decent pie.

Ⓒ *Mon–Thu, 11am–11pm; Fri–Sat, 11am–1am; Sun, 11am–10.30pm*

Balham Tup

21 Chestnut Grove, SW12

(020) 8772 0546

⊖ Balham

Like an adult version of those big rooms filled with squidgy balls that kids get to play in, except the Tup is the size of a small warehouse and it has beer instead of balls. That said, there are still quite a few balls – it shows some very bloke-friendly sport on giant TVs. It's a fun place to meet friends for drinks as it has lots of room and is pretty close to the tube. The Tup can get busy when a big match is being shown, so it's worth checking before you go if you don't fancy getting covered in beer when England lose at something they're meant to be good at.

Ⓒ *Mon–Thu, 3pm–11pm; Fri, 3pm–12am; Sat–Sun, 12pm–12am*

Food for nought

If the best things in life are free, why do we never see piles of steak and mash, with glasses of fruity rouge, sitting out on the counter with big tickets reading 'take me if you want me' on them? The truth is, London's big and expensive, so if you want to line your stomach for nothing you have to be sneaky. It pays to befriend a chef – preferably one in a big hotel, where they won't notice food slipping out occasionally. Meet your chef-with-benefits at a hotel bar at the end of his shift and tell him how hungry and skint you are. If you're really sinking fast, it sometimes pays to loiter outside **Pret a Manger** at closing time. We've fallen drunkenly over crates of unopened sandwiches before. Forget rummaging through **McDonald's** bins, though. We've tried a few times, but we could never get the padlocks off...

The Bedford

77 Bedford Hill, SW12

(020) 8682 8940

⊖ Balham

This is a massive pub but it needs the space, as The Bedford is busier than a bingo hall on pension day. Fortunately though, it has almost nothing else in common with a bingo hall on pension day. Comedy nights, live sport, good pub grub, late-night drunken dancing and boozing are all rocking on apace here, and it's a stone's throw from both an overland and a tube station. A great laugh whatever the occasion, and no need to worry about getting the come-on from an old biddy with a blotter and Robert Mugabe specs.

☻ *Times and prices vary*
depending on event

The Railway

18 Clapham High Street, SW4

(020) 7622 4077

⊖ Clapham North

A landmark pub with its giant metal fish bolted to the outside, The Railway sits right on Clapham High Street and has a roomy feel. Although sometimes lacking in atmosphere it does serve some decent Thai food, plus an interesting line in ciders. And yes, we all know cider drinking has a certain stigma attached, but these brews are of the rare, French and appley variety rather than the 79p scooter fuel type. Also, the place is right by the railway station, so after all that boozy juice you can totter off home with the minimum of fuss.

☻ *Mon–Fri & Sun, 11am–11pm;*
Sat, 11am–12am

The George

14–16 Balham Hill, SW12

(020) 8673 3104

⊖ Clapham South

Virtually nothing can beat this huge pub for crashing out on a weekend lunchtime with some papers and an icy cider or three. The sofas are strangely womb-like (not in an icky way, obviously) and the food is so comforting you could quite happily move in. Like a lot of places in South London, The George is mostly staffed by Antipodeans, beaming roundly as their beautiful tans fade in the eternal British winter, and this adds to the cheery atmosphere while also making any big sporting clash quite interesting.

☻ *Mon–Sat, 12pm–11.30pm;*
Sun, 12pm–11pm

Rook And Jackdaw

100 Balham High Road, SW12

(020) 8772 9021

⊖ Balham

'Hmmm, loads of places to sit...' is probably what you'll think when you first glance through the plate glass frontage of this pleasant central Balham pub, so as you might guess, it's a good place to rest your backside and refuel with some fine pub grub and beer. The breakfasts on Sunday are worth special attention. They operate a buffet system, so if you're really hungry and around at the right time you can be sure you won't leave unsatisfied. You can also reserve seats here for special occasions and pre-planned drinks.

☻ *Mon–Thu & Sun, 11am–11.30pm;*
Fri–Sat, 11am–1.30am

South

The Royal Oak

10 Clapham High Street, SW4
(020) 7720 5678
⊖ Clapham North

Having a drink here is like having a beer in an old friend's lounge, albeit a very rich old friend. It has a wonderfully warm and relaxed atmosphere and also boasts some of the finest pub food to be found South of the river. Their Sunday roast would've been outlawed in days gone by for being just so damn tasty you'd never have gone to church in case you didn't get that sofa seat for lunch. Having said that, you can be fairly sure of having a pleasant time whenever you choose to drink in The Royal Oak. A simple yet extremely decent pub.

🕓 *Mon–Thu, 12pm–11pm; Fri, 12pm–12am; Sat, 12am–1am; Sun, 12pm–10.30pm*

The Sun

47 Old Town, SW4
(020) 7622 4980
⊖ Clapham Common

Massive, sprawling summer hangout and winter bolthole. That's how most Aussies seem to view South London, and this popular Clapham Old Town pub has a lot in common with its surrounding area. It's good in the summer (when you can happily brulée yourself in the brief windows of sunshine) but maybe less so when there's a bit of a chill in the air. Bank Holiday weekends at The Sun are fun but can be fairly chaotic – see if you can join the queue and get served without still being there on Tuesday.

🕓 *Mon–Thu, 11am–11.30pm; Fri–Sat, 11am–12.30am; Sun, 12pm–11.30pm*

SW4

196 Clapham High Street, SW4

(020) 7498 4931

⊖ Clapham Common

In direct contradiction to the Alexandra pub located opposite, SW4 is naffer than one of those Global Hypercolor T-shirts that some of us used to bust out with shouty board shorts and yellow trainers back in junior school, but it can just about qualify as a guilty pleasure if you like neon bars advertising alcopops and music chosen by a 15-year old. OK, maybe we exaggerate its lack of any credibility, as this cleverly named bar, like so many places, can be fun with a decent bunch of mates and a table full of drinks.

☻ Mon–Thu, 11am–12am; Fri–Sat, 11am–2am; Sun, 12pm–12am

The Wheatsheaf

2 Upper Tooting Road, SW17

(020) 8672 2805

⊖ Tooting Bec

'Aiiiteelyewaatttmeeoollllmahtttyeeee'. No, not an subtitling error in a badly-dubbed film on Channel Four, but the sort of thing you may well hear at the very traditional Wheatsheaf. You see, it's the sort of pub where that man could've been sat at the bar for ten hours or ten years and you wouldn't know the difference, apart from that his lager be flat. On the plus side, if Irish hurling is your thing then you'll be sure to find some on in the back room. Coming here is an experience, especially if they've put on some 'entertainment' that evening.

☻ Mon–Thu & Sat–Sun, 11am–11pm; Fri, 11am–2am

The Clapham North

409 Clapham Road, SW9

(020) 7274 2472

⊖ Clapham North

There must be something about owning a venue in this part of London that really drives the creative juices, as here's another great example of a cleverly named boozer. But ignore the name and you'll find a very lively bar/pub with some decent grub on an interesting menu and just about every type of seating known to man. Booths, sofas, benches, square tables, high tables, low tables, round tables... You won't find any knights in shining armour to sit at them, but you will find some very easy–on–the–eye bar staff pouring drinks.

☻ Sun–Wed, 11am–12am; Thu–Sat, 11am–2am

South

CLAPHAM CLUBS

The Clapham Grand
21–25 St John's Hill, SW11
(020) 7223 6523
Clapham Junction (BR)

This is Clapham Junction's answer to the Brixton Academy, and while it's obviously not quite on a par with Bricky's legendary gig venue, you can still have a decent night out at one of its many club or gig nights. It's not too pricey, nor particularly classy, (or grand for that matter), but it's the best place to end up out of all the dubious clubs around Clapham Junction.

Mon, 7.30pm–11pm; Wed, 7pm–12am; Thu, 9.30pm–2am; Fri, 9.30pm–3am; Sat, 9.30pm–3am

Prices vary according to event

CLAPHAM CAFÉS

Café Nile
19 Clapham High Street, SW4
(020) 7622 1331
Clapham Common

You will never buy your lunch from the supermarket again once you've dined here. Situated on a busy street corner, Café Nile is a great refuge where you can grab a tasty sandwich and a coffee, all served by some very pleasant and helpful staff. Cleopatra never had it this good. Or she would have had, if her nose had been an inch longer. Or shorter. Whatever. We don't trust anyone who gets their kicks bathing in asses' milk.

Mon–Fri, 7.30am–7.30pm; Sat, 8.30am–7.30pm; Sun, 9.30am–6.30pm

Lasagne with salad, £4

Infernos
146 Clapham High Street, SW4
(020) 7720 7633
Clapham Common

Famous for providing the sort of evening that you'll either remember as one of the blackest days of your life or a thumping night out, Infernos has about as much class and credibility as Cliff Richard playing Butlins in January ('We're all going on our s-s-s-summer h-h-holidays – Jeeesus can we get some more heating in here please Roy?'). The music policy is a car crash tour through the darkest years of pop and the interior feels like a strip club, but if flashing dance floors and a drunken snog around every chromed corner sound fun then by all means join the queue.

Times and prices vary

Ditto Deli
2 Barmouth Road, SW18
(020) 8871 2586
Wandsworth Town (BR)

Situated in the heart of South London's Nappy Valley, this oddly shaped little café is a great place to enjoy a well-brewed coffee and a tasty sarnie or artistic little pastry. However, Itchy's hot tip for this place is that it's all about timing. Schedule your visit carefully to avoid hoards of braying mummies treating little Tarquins and not-so-little Henriettas to an afternoon out – they'll take up half the café and the kids spend most of the time crying. Oh yeah, we're full of maternal instinct, us.

Mon–Sat, 7.30am–7.30pm; Sun, 8.30am–4pm

Ham and cheese croissant, £1.75

CLAPHAM RESTAURANTS

The Blithe Spirit

157 Balham High Road, SW12

(020) 8772 0082

⊖ Balham

This is one of Balham's classiest places to eat and drink and it has the bonus of a large outside terrace for summer time soirées. The food is better than average and the décor is pretty smart, but without making it feel too much like you might have wandered into Liberace's boudoir. An Itchy favourite for some sophisticated drinks in South London.

🅲 *Mon–Wed, 11am–11pm; Thu & Sun, 11am–12am; Fri–Sat, 11am–1am*

🍽 *Sunday roast (beef, lamb or pork), £9.50*

💲 *£11.50*

Eco

162 Clapham High Street, SW4

(020) 7978 1108

⊖ Clapham Common

Pizza places are numerous in South London but this is one of the best. It's great if you're meeting up with mates for dinner due to the long tables, but it can feel a bit impersonal. A takeaway option is also available which is a good plan if the sun is shining on the nearby common – instant al fresco dining. We just hope you can tell the difference between an ant and a bit of black pepper on your margherita.

🅲 *Mon–Thu, 12pm–4pm & 6pm–11pm; Fri, 12pm–4pm & 6pm–11.30pm; Sat, 12pm–11.30pm; Sun, 12pm–11pm*

🍽 *Goats' cheese pizza, £8.25*

💲 *£10.95*

Chatkhara

15 Upper Tooting Road, SW17

(020) 8682 2519

⊖ Tooting Bec

The late-night revellers come from far and wide to eat at Chatkhara, and it's all down to one very important thing – the chicken tikka roll. First they'll slap a lump of freshly-kneaded dough into a tandoori oven to make a naan bread, then they'll cook some juicy lumps of spicy chicken and then, after asking if you want chilli sauce four times, the whole lot will be combined in a glorious tube of salad, bread and meat. Go, seek it out, and you will not be disappointed.

🅲 *Times vary*

🍽 *Chicken tikka roll, £2.50*

💲 *Not licensed*

Fish in a Tie

105 Falcon Road, SW11

(020) 7924 1913

⊖ Clapham Junction (BR)

Hiding on a street round the back of the station does nothing to deter people from packing this joint out every night of the week. It's got all the ingredients that make eating out fun – great atmosphere, candles, friendly cute staff and great food at ridiculously cheap prices. The menu doesn't change too much but the regulars like it that way – try the crab in choux pastry starter, and the duck for mains.

🕒 Mon–Fri; 12pm–3pm & 6pm–12am; Sat, 12pm–12am; Sun, 12pm–11pm

🍴 Breast of duck in honey and ginger sauce, £6.95

💷 £9.95

Little Bay

228 York Road, SW11

(020) 7223 4080

⊖ Clapham Junction (BR)

There aren't too many restaurants around that let you eat in a treehouse while looking down at a warbling opera singer. It can get hot and stuffy up high when it's busy, but this little place just ten minutes walk from Clapham Junction is worth the trek. It's so cheap you'll wonder whether they've made a mistake – could mussels in white wine really cost less than a fiver? The atmosphere's a feast in itself. Book ahead if you want a good spot at the normal time.

🕒 Mon–Fri, 12pm–11pm; Sat, 12pm–10.30pm; Sun, 12pm–10pm

🍴 All mains, £5.95 before 7pm, £7.95 after

💷 £10.90

The Frog and Forget-Me-Not

32 The Pavement, SW4

(020) 7622 5230

⊖ Clapham Common

On Tuesdays, people flock to the Frog for the legendary pub quiz, having stuffed their faces with the cheap and gorgeous Thai food. We love the huge, comfy sofas, the central bar with its rowdy Aussie staff and the general 'playing in your living room' type atmosphere. It's better in the winter in our opinion, as in summertime there isn't any outside seating so people flock to The Sun down the road, but you can't beat it for comfort when it's cold outside.

🕒 Mon–Fri, 4pm–12am; Sat, 12pm–12am; Sun, 12pm–10.30pm

🍴 Sunday roast, £7.95

💷 £12.50

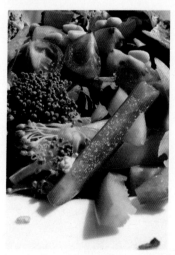

South

Golden Curry

131 Clapham High Street, SW4

(020) 7720 9558

⊖ Clapham Common

A cut above your average curry house in both décor and price, and the food is thoroughly tasty but occasionally a bit boring (who wants their naan delivered in neat little slices?) Sure, it's nice enough and the staff are friendly, but it lacks that 'curry house' vibe – the Golden Curry is more like a standard restaurant, which may be a plus point for some. It does boast a good location though, so you could do a lot worse than stop here for pre or post-drink food. Takeaway is also available.

🕔 *Times vary*

🍴 *Chicken korma, £5.25*

💰 *£9*

Pizza Metro

64 Battersea Rise, SW11

(020) 7228 3812

⊖ Clapham Junction (BR)

Metro, metro, metro.... You know, it seems that whenever anyone wants to make something sound new and futuristic, they call it Metro. Newspapers; underground lines; hell, the northerners even tried it with a shopping centre in Newcastle. Frankly, fellas, you're fooling no-one. Which is why Itchy gives a deep sigh of relief whenever we head into this old school pizzeria. No fancy shenanigans here, just pizza served up by the metre on big trays as diners pack it down.

🕔 *Tue–Fri, 6pm–11pm; Sat, 12pm–11pm; Sun, 12pm–10.30pm*

🍴 *Diavola, £8.50*

💰 *£12.50*

Sea Cow

57 Clapham High Street, SW4

(020) 7622 1537

⊖ Clapham North/Clapham Common

Does it sell beef or rare water–dwelling mammals? Neither actually, the Sea Cow is a fish and chip shop (and fishmonger) that's had its roe fertilised by the genes of an alpha cod to make the classiest chippy in South London. You won't find any week-old battered sausages being slowly radiated to nothing in a hot glass bread bin or Vicky Pollard scooping your chips into yesterday's *Daily Sport* here, it's fish and chip heaven. A fine plaice to eat.

🕔 *Tue–Sat, 12pm–10.30pm; Sun, 12pm–10pm*

🍴 *Cod and chips, £8*

💰 *£11.50*

BOROUGH

Roast

The Floral Hall, Stoney Street, SE1
(020) 7940 1300
⊖ London Bridge

Get your parents or your other half to treat you if you're planning to check out this place. Overlooking the market, Roast promises the best of British food, cooked to perfection and focusing on meat, meat and more meat. A top notch steak for two will cost you just over £40 but it's so damn good the taste will last months in your memory.

🕒 Mon–Fri, 7am–10am, 12pm–3pm & 5.30pm–11pm; Sat, 8am–11pm, 11.30am–4pm & 6pm–11pm; Sun, 12pm–4pm
🍴 Spit roast pheasant, £17.50
💷 £14

Village East

171 Bermondsey Street, SE1
(020) 7357 6082
⊖ London Bridge

Borough Market is awash with stalls serving up good food, but what if you're in the area and you fancy something a bit fancy or a place to rest your shopped-out feet? Village East is a new hang out for the arty crowd and fashion folk that flock to sip the extra-special cocktails which are big business here. A good eating, meeting and drinking gaff, and the staff really know their bellinis from their Bollinger as well.

🕒 Mon–Fri, 12pm–3.30pm & 6pm–10pm; Sat–Sun, 12pm–4pm & 6pm–10pm
🍴 Roasted monkfish tail, chives and ginger, basil coulis and lentils, £14
💷 £14

The Rose

123 Snowfields, SE1
(020) 7378 6660
⊖ London Bridge

A gloriously rustic pub situated slap bang in the middle of the otherwise largely barren streets round London Bridge. With the log fire going it's most likely warmer than your bed (depending on who you share it with, obviously) and the décor is really interesting, albeit rather eclipsed by the gorgeous bar staff. The Rose is well worth going slightly out of your way to locate if you find yourself travelling through London Bridge for one reason or another and can't face a gassy pint in the ubiquitous, sweaty train station pub.

🕒 Mon–Sat, 11am–11pm; Sun, 11am–10.30pm

GREENWICH

Crown and Greyhound

73 Dulwich Village, SE21
(020) 8299 4976
⊖ North Dulwich (BR)

A lovely place that has retained the feel of a traditional pub, yet has a clean, airy feel in the more up-to-date dining area with its open kitchen. They serve brilliant Sunday lunches, when plates from the carvery brim with tender pork or beef. Worth a visit in the summer when they have BBQs in the garden. Admittedly, you may have to be more aggressive than a baseball-capped youth in a Golf to grab a table, but it'll be worth the fight.

🕒 Mon–Sat, 11am–11pm; Sun, 11am–10.30pm

South

WATERLOO

Anchor & Hope

36 The Cut, SE1

(020) 7928 9898

⊖ Waterloo/Southwark

If we woke up one day to hear that there was a massive asteroid heading for earth, what would Itchy do? Well, apart from the things we can't say in print, we'd probably spend an evening here, tucking into London's best pub food, drinking red wine out of little tumblers, and wishing we'd followed up on our childhood intentions of learning how to fly a spaceship.

🕓 *Mon, 5pm–12.30am; Tue–Sat, 11am–11pm; Sun, 12.30pm–5.30pm; Food, Mon, 6pm–10.30pm; Tue–Sat 12.30pm–2pm & 6pm–10.30pm; Sun, 2pm (single sitting)*

The Duke Of Sussex

23 Bayliss Road, SE1

(020) 7928 6814

⊖ Waterloo/Southwark

An old-school Sarf Lahndan boozer of the highest order that not only has some of the friendliest Cockernee barstaff that LDN has to offer, but can also boast one of the most entertaining sights available to a Friday evening reveller in London – drunken karaoke. Not just drunken karaoke, but horrendously bad drunken karaoke. Itchy has seen good men forever tarnished by performances of *The Cheeky Song* by The Cheeky Girls. Then again some of the singing isn't bad at all, but that's no fun, is it? Humiliation is far more entertaining and if you can't stand the noise then there's a pool table next door.

🕓 *Mon–Sun, 12pm–12am*

Cubana

48 Lower Marsh, SE1

(020) 7928 8778

⊖ Waterloo/Southwark

So dedicated to recreating that authentic Cuban feel are they that weekend evenings see people perching on rickety chairs and tables and congregating around the bins in the dirty car park that adjoins the venue in true pursuit of the shanty town experience. The inside is a multi-layered bar full of trendy young things swilling back cocktails and eating the selection of hispanic food. It can get unpleasantly rammed at weekends, and why you'd pay the after-hours entry fee here, when The Duke over the road's open late for free, God knows. Still, they do a nice cocktail.

🕓 *Mon–Tue, 12pm–12am; Wed–Thu, 12pm–1am; Fri, 12pm–3am; Sat, 5pm–3am*

South

VAUXHALL

The Riverside
5 St George's Wharf, SW8
(020) 7735 8129
⊖ Vauxhall

On a list of gastropub clichés, The Riverside would have more ticks than a tramp's pet sheep in a Biblical plague of fleas. They've gone for wide appeal by relying on the tried and trusted, but sadly border on being bland. Itchy found the amazing pork to be a beacon of light amid an otherwise safe, beige menu, but the service was outstanding.

◉ Mon–Fri, 11am–12am; Sat–Sun, 10am–12am; Food, Mon–Fri, 11am–10.30pm; Sat–Sun, 10.30am–10.30pm
🍴 Pork in bacon with champ, £11.50
💷 £13.95

STOCKWELL

The Swan
215 Clapham Road, SW9
(020) 7978 9778
⊖ Stockwell

Some bods at Itchy Towers look back at nights out here with teary-eyed nostalgia – 'the people, the food, the drinks, the cover bands...'. The rest of us have to fetch the cold water and smelling salts to knock some sense into them, as The Swan is the sort of place you'll either love or hate. It's brash, cheesy and the cover acts that regularly take the stage provide entertainment of the highest class, so go once as you might just find your nirvana.

◉ Mon–Sun, 7pm–late
💷 Free–£6

LONDON BRIDGE

SeOne
11 Stainer Street, SE1
(020) 7407 1617
⊖ London Bridge

Clubs harder than an Eskimo in a seal sanctuary. SeOne has five vast indoor festival spaces ranging from the very swish Deep Blue room to massive, under-arch dancefloors. It's the sort of place we would hide if the orcs of Mordor were coming to get us. Which they will be, because there's more bass in this place than in the whole of the North Atlantic. Glowbugs should check out Echo System nights for true psy-trance, and Itchy doffs its trilby to the legendary cult Hat Club.

◉ Times and prices vary

Vodka Revolution
95–96 Clapham High Street, SW4
(020) 7720 6642
⊖ Stockwell

No, not an obscure historical footnote referring to an ancient Russian battle for democracy, but a popular chain bar that specialises in the serving of fermented potatoes and charging you quite highly for the pleasure. It could be a slightly under-sized car showroom were it not for the seats, but it's open 'til late and if you like a boogie with your fermented potato and Coke beverage then this is somewhere you'll enjoy. You can get leathered on over 30 varieties of vodka here as well – if that's not mixing your drinks then we don't know what is.

◉ Times and prices vary

Test of moral fibre

ALRIGHT, SO WE'RE ALL SUPPOSED TO BE EATING ETHICALLY NOWADAYS. BUT WHAT WE WANT TO KNOW IS WHETHER ANY OF THE MONKEYS THAT BANG ON ABOUT THIS STUFF HAVE EVER TRIED IT OUT WHEN PICKING UP SOME POST-PUB STOMACH FILLERS. IT'S A BLOODY NIGHTMARE. OBSERVE:

Illustration by Si Clark, www.si-clark.co.uk

1 **Food miles –** According to some environmental fascist or other, it's not ecologically friendly to eat stuff that's been flown across the world when you could chomp on courgettes grown much closer to home. Not according to our friendly burger van, however.

Itchy: 'Excuse me, but how many food miles has that quarter pounder done?'

Burger man: 'What?'

Itchy: 'How many miles has it travelled to end up here?'

Burger man: 'Ten miles, mate. Straight from Lidl to this spot.'

Itchy: 'But what about where it came from originally? What about the sourcing?'

Burger man: 'Saucing? I've got ketchup and mustard, you cheeky sod. And it's free, not like him down the road and his "10p-a-sachet" bollocks, now you gonna buy this burger or what?'

'Reckon you could catch enough fish for all the UK's chippies using a fishing rod?'

2 **Sustainability –** It's not meant to be the done thing to eat fish caught in a way that stops our scaly friends reproducing fast enough to prevent their numbers dropping. Sadly, no-one's told our local chippy.

Itchy: 'Is your cod line-caught?'

Chippy owner: 'Yeah, it's caught mate. How else do you reckon it comes from the sea?'

Itchy: 'No, I'm asking if it was caught using a fishing rod.'

Chippy owner: 'You reckon you could catch enough fish for all the UK's chippies using a fishing rod?'

Itchy: 'Erm, no...'

Chippy owner: 'Right, well there's your answer then.'

Itchy: '...but, you know that you should only really eat fish from sustainable sources don't you?'

Chippy owner: 'Oh yeah? According to who? The media? Reckon all that coke they're on's organic? Produced locally, is it?'

Itchy: 'Well, it's not always possible to consume entirely ethically...'

Chippy owner: 'My point exactly. One cod and chips then is it?'

Riverside pubs

THE THAMES IS THE HEART OF LONDON. SO THERE AIN'T NO BETTER WAY TO TAKE IN THE CAPITAL THAN BY VISITING ONE OF THE BOOZERS BY ITS COFFEE-COLOURED WATERS

The Prospect of Whitby

57 Wapping Wall, E1

(020) 7481 1095

⊖ Wapping

Anywhere once known as 'Devil's Tavern' has to be worth a trek into Wapping. Once the haunt of smugglers and pirates, it still has gallows outside in memory of the bad old days. The interior looks suspiciously like reclaimed timber from old ships, and the terrace looks out onto the Thames at its most vast and impressive.

The Dove

19 Upper Mall, W6

(020) 8748 9474

⊖ Hammersmith

In olde Hammersmith, minutes from the Amsterdam-esque Chiswick Mall and the tidal island of Chiswick Eyot, the Dove's a boozer for all seasons. In winter you can nestle in the cosy interior with one of the dogs that are always knocking around, while in summer, the balcony has cracking views of Hammersmith Bridge.

The Anchor

34 Park Street, SE1

(020) 7407 1577

⊖ London Bridge

You might need a cattle prod to thrash your way through the herds of tourists milling around outside this place, but once inside, there's room at the inn for all. Grab a roast beef sandwich from the carvery and revel in the pub's situation in the middle of the schizophrenic Bankside, where historic London clashes with naked profiteering.

The Gipsy Moth

60 Greenwich Street, SE10

(0871) 332 5319

⊖ Cutty Sark (DLR)

Alright, so you can't actually see the Thames from here, but you can sort of smell it. Nestling in touristy Greenwich, the Gipsy Moth is fortunately more spacious than its namesake, the shoebox in which Sir Francis Chichester circumnavigated the globe. There are some decent ales, and it's especially pleasant in summer.

West

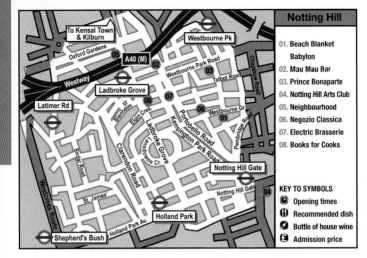

Notting Hill

01. Beach Blanket Babylon
02. Mau Mau Bar
03. Prince Bonaparte
04. Notting Hill Arts Club
05. Neighbourhood
06. Negozio Classica
07. Electric Brasserie
08. Books for Cooks

KEY TO SYMBOLS

- 🕐 Opening times
- 🍴 Recommended dish
- 🍷 Bottle of house wine
- 💷 Admission price

NOTTING HILL BARS

Beach Blanket Babylon

45 Ledbury Road, W11

(020) 7229 2907

⊖ Notting Hill Gate

Totter over a piratical chain bridge to park yourself on a bejewelled throne built into the wall, or lose yourself in the mosaic walls and imagine you're anyone from Marie Antoinette to Dumbledore. Even the toilets here are mad, with elf-sized cubicles and windy passageways. Drinks though are far too expensive to make this fantasy land worth an all-night stop, so sip that cocktail like it's the last you'll ever have and move on.

🕐 Mon–Fri, 12pm–12am; Sat, 10.30am–12am; Sun, 12pm–10.30pm

Mau Mau Bar

265 Portobello Road, W11

(020) 7792 2043

⊖ Notting Hill Gate

With bags of personality – although some might be a little too toff at times – this live music venue hits all the right notes for a loud night out with the 'cool' people. It gets quite crowded at weekends but during the day Mau Mau's comfy sofas are a great place to chill, sip coffee and scan the papers, and they book some great gigs. You might want to give the open mic nights a miss though. There's only so many Chelsea girls singing dreary acoustic ballads one can handle without vomming into an overpriced pint.

🕐 Mon–Sat, 11am–11pm; Sun, 12pm–10.30pm

Ruby & Sequoia

6–8 All Saints Road, W11

(020) 7243 6363

⊖ Ladbroke Grove

The people here might be far too cool for school, but the Notting Hill glitterati are loving the new hot spot from the Ruby Lounge guys. The restaurant-quality food is served in diner–style booths and we're a great fan of the funky retro wallpaper. When you're done with your braised rabbit entrée, (oh yeah, there's no half measures here), head downstairs to the Sequoia basement where the DJ spins it hard late into the night under the perspex lights. A great spot for a rendez-vous with a special someone. Just bring the credit card.

☻ *Mon–Thu, 6pm–12.30am; Fri, 6pm–2am; Sat, 11am–2am; Sun, 11am–11pm*

NOTTING HILL PUBS

Bumpkin

209 Westbourne Park Road, W11

(020) 7243 9818

⊖ Westbourne Park

It's not like a real country pub. Not really. There are no sticky floors, filthy carpets or old men falling asleep at the bar. But the brand new Bumpkin takes the nicer aspects of country pubbage and pulls them together to create a rather overpriced reminder of that lunchtime pit stop you had in the middle of nowhere on the family trip to Norfolk when you were five. Serving traditional British food, it's quaint enough if you're after something different.

☻ *Mon–Sat, 5.30pm–12am; Sun, 12pm–5pm; Food, Tue–Fri, 12pm–3pm*

Prince Bonaparte

80 Chepstow Road, W2

(020) 7313 9491

⊖ Notting Hill Gate

When winter nips at our cute little noses, we here at Itchy love to stumble upon a pub with a roaring fire – and like this watering hole's namesake, we're willing to fight to get a seat beside it (we mean that our willingness to fight is similar to his – we have no idea what his opinion on being near the fire was). Luckily, the Bonaparte is big enough that you can loiter until an unsuspecting fireside dweller goes to the loo, and then pounce. The beers are average, (Carlsberg, Stella, etc) but the wine list is fab, as is the food coming from the open kitchen. Bit loud at weekends but in general, we love it here.

☻ *Mon–Sat, 12pm–11pm; Sun, 12pm–10.30pm*

NOTTING HILL CLUBS

Blag Club

1st Floor, 68 Notting Hill Gate, W11

(020) 7243 0123

⊖ Notting Hill Gate

Mullets and cut-off denim numbers at the ready. Oh, and 'blag' a platinum card from somewhere before you leave, because unless your budget stretches to cocktails at a tenner a pop, you won't last long in this place. It used to be cool when it was the Hill's only late-night gay bar, but now it heaves with snootiness, weird hairdos and a rather pointless moving display featuring marine life. Unless you're pissed and you've pulled a rich piece of totty with more money than sense, forget about it.

Ⓒ *Wed–Sat, 7.30pm–1am*

Neighbourhood

12 Acklam Road, W10

(020) 7524 7979

⊖ Westbourne Park/Ladbroke Grove

For three years this superclub near Portobello Road has been drawing the masses with its massive, triple-stack Funktion1 soundsystem, 'understated' two-floor space and fab visual aesthetics. Everyone's played here, from Damon Albarn to The Libertines (they even made it to the gig), through Craaaaaiiiiig David and Corinne Bailey-Rae to REM, and the host of international DJs create a flavour you won't forget. Unless you get completely off your tits, obviously, in which case you might well forget the flavour. Or it might be tainted by sick. Party on.

Ⓒ *Wed–Sat, 8pm–2am; Sun, 5pm–12am*

The Gate

87 Notting Hill Gate, W11

(020) 7727 9007

⊖ Notting Hill Gate

So you want a homemade pan-European tapas menu with goats' cheese crostini and beetroot purée? You want to drool, glittery-eyed over the cornmeal-coated squid with smoked chilli dipping sauce? Well hold your horses, because it gets better than that. Head for dinner here first before the DJ packs the place out with hip tunes, or the salsa dance classes take over (aided by a few of those top-notch cocktails). It's got all you could want and more. Used to be a bit of a secret, but even now that people know about it, it's still cool. Which makes it a rarity in this part of town.

Ⓒ *Mon–Sun, 6pm–1am*

Notting Hill Arts Club

21 Notting Hill Gate, W11

(020) 7460 4459

⊖ Notting Hill Gate

We haven't seen this many gruesome-looking tools in a basement since Freddy Kruger gave us the guided tour of his kiddy-butchering torture chamber in *Nightmare on Elm Street*. Still, if you can stand the slant towards pretentious indie pop types trying to look hip through greasy fringes, you'll have yourself a rocking time in the most popular club on the block. Drinks are pretty cheap, the live bands are usually awesome, and we love Death Disco, when the legendary Alan McGee spins choons smoother than his head.

Ⓒ *Mon–Wed, 6pm–1am; Thu–Fri, 6pm–2am; Sat, 4pm–2am; Sun, 4pm–1am*

NOTTING HILL CAFÉS

Books for Cooks

4 Blenheim Crescent, W11

(020) 7221 1992

Ladbroke Grove

Forget the expensive sarnies in those chain book store cafés. Books for Cooks do it properly, with thousands of cookbooks sitting beside a test kitchen, where you're invited to put theory into practice. Every day, at tables squished into cosy alcoves between the bookshelves, you can sample gorgeous lunches, home-baked cakes and coffee, until everything runs out. Fab for a Saturday afternoon away from the market, cookery classes are also available.

Tue–Sat, 10am–6pm

Slice of cake, £2

Negozio Classica

283 Westbourne Grove, W11

(020) 7034 0005

Notting Hill Gate

Wine and cheese freaks unite – we've found your Italian heaven on a leafy street in London. Looking like just one more of the boutiques littering the area, Negozio is actually part of an international company, so this lot know their stuff. If you can't tell your Merlots from your Brunellos you'll have fun learning, with a flat rate corkage of £4.50 on the shelf prices. Try the parma ham and some of the well-chosen cheeses to enhance the flavours. Cheese-tastic.

Mon–Thu, 11am–11pm; Fri, 11am–12am; Sat, 9am–12am

Tuscan cured ham with rocket and parmesan, £9.95

Café Grove

253a Portobello Road, W11

(020) 7243 1094

Ladbroke Grove

During the summer, this is Notting Hill at its finest, and if you can bag one of the tables on the terrace for a cooked breakfast, overlooking the bustling market, chances are you'll want to stay there all day. European dishes, from hefty, gut-busting breakfasts to tempting tapas make up a varied menu, and it gains extra points for the fact that the pushchair-wielding Notting Hill mums can't get their screaming offspring up the stairs. This firm local fave is all the better for it.

Mon–Sat, 9.30am–6pm; Sun, 10.30am–6pm

Deep sea pancake, £6.90

Progreso

156 Portobello Road, W11

(020) 7985 0304

Notting Hill Gate

Stocking only fairtrade produce, its individuality makes for a refreshing change from the omnipresent chain bars. Coffee is served in big, handle-less mugs and there are loads of organic juices, soups, chunky cookies, and cakes to tempt you. The basement is perfect for escaping the bustle of Portobello market, taking some quiet time or having secret liaisons with a work colleague. It also boasts free table football and a huge bed-like cushion. Get cosy.

Mon–Thu, 7am–6.30pm; Fri–Sat, 7am–7pm; Sun, 8.30am–7pm

Crème fraîche and bacon baguette, £3.75

NOTTING HILL RESTAURANTS

Crazy Homies

125 Westbourne Park Road, W2

(020) 7727 6771

↔ Westbourne Park

The name had us a bit excited, with visions of *Grand Theft Auto* style characters planning bank raids in unmarked Transit vans, but if the truth be told, you'd probably have to be a little bit of a crazy homie to go back twice. It's just OK. The Mexican food is decent, but service is a bit slow and the place gets rowdy – the potent margaritas are probably to blame.

Ⓒ *Mon–Sun, 6pm–12am*

🍴 *Melting pork picadillo, £8.95*

💰 *£15*

The Electric Brasserie

191 Portobello Road, W11

(020) 7908 9696

↔ Notting Hill Gate

Prepare to wait a while on a Sunday – the queues go out of the door – but this is one of Itchy's fave spots to go for the kind of high-class brunch you'll be hard pressed to find anywhere else outside of Manhattan. We loved the decadence of creamed tomatoes on toast and the perfect eggs Benedict. What's more, the staff are so hot we were tempted to spill our lattes just to get their attention. Divine post-pay day Notting Hill grub – but most definitely not for 'poor week'.

Ⓒ *Mon–Sat, 8pm–12am; Sun, 10am–11pm*

🍴 *Full Electric breakfast, £10*

💰 *£20*

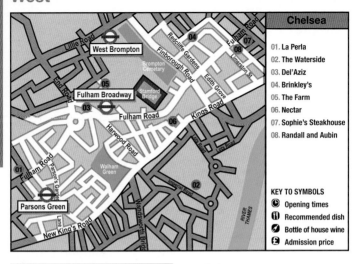

Chelsea

01. La Perla
02. The Waterside
03. Del'Aziz
04. Brinkley's
05. The Farm
06. Nectar
07. Sophie's Steakhouse
08. Randall and Aubin

KEY TO SYMBOLS
- 🕐 Opening times
- 🍴 Recommended dish
- 🍷 Bottle of house wine
- 💷 Admission price

CHELSEA BARS

Bar 190

The Gore Hotel, 190 Queen's Gate, SW7
(020) 7584 660
⊖ Gloucester Road

A hit with visiting telly and movie fashionistas, everything about Bar 190 is worked out to complement the events at the Royal Albert Hall. The huge, long bar hosts a multitude of slick, eager to please staff, all super-keen to provide you with 16 types of brandy, 15 different sparkly champagnes and service with an even sparklier smile. Not to mention a toss of that shiny, highlighted hair. Watch out for the American tourists grumbling on about the poor exchange rate. Suckers.

🕐 *Mon–Sun, 5pm–11pm*

La Perla

803 Fulham Road, SW6
(020) 7471 4895
⊖ Parsons Green

Tequila fans, here's a place where you can knock 'em back while sober and not feel like a weirdo. From Blanco, (young and un-aged), to Anejo, (aged for over a year), there's enough here to help you soak up those juicy fajitas, tortillas and quesadillas. The terracotta walls and Mexican beer posters all add to the general ambience, and after a few tequilas we were sure to keep one eye out for a long-haired, wandering mariachi with a guitar case full of guns, asking around the bar for a man called Bucho.

🕐 *Mon–Fri, 5pm–11pm; Sat, 12pm–11pm; Sun, 12pm–10.30pm*

The Waterside

Riverside Tower, Imperial Wharf, SW6

(020) 7371 0802

⊖ Fulham Broadway

Relatively new, this Youngs addition to the splurge of gastro-pubs overlooking London's finest scenes is a welcome treat. Close to the pier, it's one for those Chelsea dwellers who like their dinner with a little less attitude and a little more style. Itchy visited on a cold, rainy day, but eating one of the best roasts we've gobbled outside of gran's house, we were more than happy to chat while watching the rain spatter the banks of the Thames. A bottle of wine or two by the crackling fire was the perfect way to round up a Sunday afternoon.

🕒 *Mon–Sat, 10.30am–12am; Sun, 10.30am–10.30pm*

CHELSEA PUBS

Admiral Codrington

17 Mossop Street, SW3

(020) 7581 0005

⊖ South Kensington

The Cod, as it's affectionately known, is a firm fave with Euan Blair and other socialites in the area, but still retains quite an unpretentious aura. We were impressed by the mammoth wine and champers menu, although you'll need to have something to celebrate if you're staying. The food's a bit pricey, (a roast dinner plus wine will set you back more than £15) but the quality, wooden seats and comfy demeanour will win you over. In the summer, their retractable roof is pretty damn cool too.

🕒 *Mon–Sun, 11am–11pm*

The Duke's Head

8 Lower Richmond Road, SW15

(020) 8788 2552

⊖ Putney Bridge

It's amazing what a quick spruce can do, and trust us, they would have had to do more to this boring old boozer than stock up on Mr Sheen and hire the local bob-a-jobbing Boy Scouts for the afternoon. Luckily, they've done it good 'n' proper, and what used to be uninspiring is now quite a find, with a dazzling river view, tapas, cocktails, a basement bar and oodles of natural light upstairs. They've got good grub too – we loved the salmon fishcakes and on our visit the waiter was so pleased to see us we were almost disturbed.

🕒 *Mon–Thu & Sun, 11am–12am; Fri–Sat, 11am–1am*

West

Finch's

190 Fulham Road, SW10

(020) 7351 5043

⊖ Earl's Court

Oozing sport from every pore, this old Victorian pub has come a long way since the ladies floated past in their big frocks on the arms of football-oblivious, top hat-wearing gentlemen. Still, its gorgeous original tiling, bright stained glass skylight and tasty handmade chips mean that when the multitude of screens are off or on mute (and that goes for the fans as well), it's not a bad place to while away a few hours and sample the tasty regular Youngs beers. And for that big game? Well, you'll have a whale of a time, but you'd better get in early if you want a seat.

🕒 *Mon–Sat, 11am–12am; Sun, 12pm–12am*

Kavanagh's

92 Old Brompton Road, SW7

(020) 7584 6886

⊖ South Kensington

Seedy and tired basement craphole to some, cracking old-school live music joint to others – whatever you make of Kavanagh's, the locals seem to revel in its smoky depths. We'd probably recommend you don't eat here, since the fish and chips we had were quite possibly the worst we've ever tasted, but for necking a few pints, catching a good gig and watching the live sport on a huge screen, it does the job just fine. It's an easygoing sort of a place, and makes a good meeting point for a night with a few mates.

🕒 *Mon–Wed, 11am–11pm; Thu–Sat, 11am–2am; Sun, 12pm–12.30am*

The Hollywood Arms

45 Hollywood Road, SW10

(020) 7349 7840

⊖ Earl's Court/West Brompton

Just like the scabby, real life Hollywood Boulevard, this residential strip off the bustling Fulham Road has many charms, although, unlike in LA, none of them wear fishnets and call you 'sugar'. On the same sweet street as the popular Brinkley's, the recently refurbed Hollywood Arms is a candlelit cove of comfy sofas, smiley staff and an eager-to-impress chef. They've buffed up the menu – expect top-notch burgers as well as spiffing Sunday roasts, and upstairs is so cosy you'll want to take your clothes off and snuggle under a spare tablecloth. But maybe best not to.

🕒 *Mon–Sun, 10am–12am*

CHELSEA CLUBS

Crazy Larry's

533 Kings Road, SW10

(020) 7376 5555

⊖ Fulham Broadway

Aggressive door staff, arrogant punters and sticky floors – not to mention ruddy-faced rugby boys trying to pull bottle-blonde daddy's girls. The Kings Road might not be the best of places to hang out when the sun's up, but when it goes down it's worse. There are too many other places round here to waste a moment of your life in this dive. You'd have to be as crazy as whoever Larry was to venture in here.

🕒 *Thu–Sat, 9pm–2.30am; open for private parties during the week; admission prices vary, guest list available*

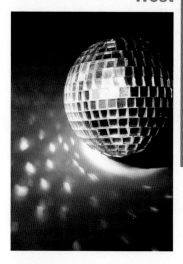

CHELSEA CAFÉS

Cambio de Tercio

163 Old Brompton Road, SW5

(020) 7244 8970

⊖ Gloucester Road

If you're looking for somewhere cute and sweet to hand feed your latest lover from a hot plate of titillating tapas, this is your place. Sure it's a bit out of the way but the best places are always off the beaten track. Watch out for the weird 'sittings' rule – you can sit at either 7pm or 9pm for your dinner – and some of the dishes may be a little on the stingy side, but you won't get a better slice of Spain down Chelsea way.

🕒 *Mon–Sun, 11am–2pm & 7pm–11.30pm*

🍴 *Segovian-style roasted suckling pig, £15.50*

Chakalaka

136 Upper Richmond Road, SW15

(020) 8789 5696

⊖ East Putney

We love the name, more than anything. Tell your mates you're meeting at Chakalaka and challenge them not to do a little dance, Bruce Forsyth-style, across the floor. Serving up steaming plates of South African grub, this cosy little place welcomes in weary walkers and the staff are more than happy to answer your annoying questions about what the hell most items on the menu actually consist of. If in doubt, go for the steak, but the lamb bobotie is worth a scoff.

🕒 *Mon–Fri, 6pm–10.45pm; Sat, 12pm–10.45pm; Sun, 12pm–10pm*

🍴 *Springbok loin, £17.95*

West

Del'Aziz

24–28 Vanston Place, SW6

(020) 7386 0086

⊖ Fulham Broadway

Dried mulberries anyone? If fancy fruits aren't your thing then this bakery/café/takeaway/deli/brasserie will still be worth the visit. The food is all freshly made on site, and has a North African/Eastern Mediterranean edge. Expect meze platters and all kinds of interesting cheeses and pastries to get your waistline bulging. For a quick snack, squeeze your chinos onto the canteen-style benches and salivate over the cakes, meats and gourmet treats, all of which can be packed up so you can take them home with you.

© Mon–Sun, 7am–7pm

⊕ Bruschettas, £3.50

CHELSEA RESTAURANTS

Brinkley's

47 Hollywood Road, SW10

(020) 7351 1683

⊖ Fulham Broadway

There aren't many joints around where you can glug wine without depending on the Bank of Mum and Dad, but here you can enjoy your vino at shop prices. In Chelsea, no less. We love the friendly, unpretentious staff, and the chance that Madge might walk in any minute – she lives just down the road.

© Mon–Sat, 5pm–11pm; Sun, 12pm–10.30pm; Food, Mon–Sat, 6pm–11.30pm; Sun, 12pm–10.30pm

⊕ Brinkley's burger with fried onions, chips and rocket, £11

❷ £7.50

The Little French Restaurant

18 Hogarth Place, SW5

(020) 7244 6082

⊖ Earl's Court

A little French restaurant (who'd have guessed?), but unlike with a lot of other such little French restaurants in London, this one actually picks you up with an 'ooh la la' and whisks you off to a different region with every mouthful. The food is fab and authentic, and considering the location, surprisingly good value. Most mains are under a tenner and the most expensive wine is just £20. Try the generous coq au vin for your dinner and don't skimp on the crème brulee for pud. Keep this a secret – we dare you.

© Mon–Sun, 6pm–11pm

⊕ Coq au vin, £8.25

Cactus Blue

86 Fulham Road, SW3

(020) 7395 5801

⊖ South Kensington

An impressive venue outside and in – the owners employed a Native American artist from Santa Fe to mix the tastes and colours from South West America into more than just the food. A mixture of Creole, Cajun and Hispanic dishes await, although Itchy was blown away by the roast dinner, during which a whole joint of perfectly cooked beef was placed before us, with a trough of vegetables fit for a king. And we've never had such an awesome Bloody Mary in London.

© Mon–Sat, 5pm–12am; Sun, 5pm–11pm

⊕ Roast beef dinner for 4, £65

❷ £14

The Farm

18 Farm Lane, SW6

(020) 7381 3331

⊖ Fulham Broadway

In a land where any pub serving food can pass themselves off as a gastropub, it's refreshing to see there are still a few that deserve the accolade. With its squishy sofas and an open fire, The Farm beckons you in like your mum on Christmas Day and invites you to curl up and be spoiled. French food in traditional English surroundings, fine wines and good beers make this farm no place for animals.

© *Mon–Fri, 12pm–12am; Sat, 10am–12am; Sun, 10am–11pm*

⊕ *Grilled rib eye steak with bEarnaise sauce and chips, £14.50*

❷ *£12.50*

Randall and Aubin

333 Fulham Road, SW10

(020) 7823 3515

⊖ Fulham Broadway

This is part two of Randall and Aubin's empire – the other is in Soho. It's a pretty low-key affair when you step through the door, though the food is anything but. The blurb states this place 'skips to a beat of its own' and they've hit the nail on the head. They don't specialise in anything in particular but expect fresh seafood, an array of interesting meats and a few traditional dishes thrown in for good measure. A good place to take the parents if they're visiting.

© *Mon–Sat, 12pm–12am; Sun, 12pm–10.30pm*

⊕ *Salmon and haddock fishcakes, £9*

❷ *£13.95*

Nectar

562 Kings Road, SW6

(020) 7326 7450

⊖ Parsons Green

A stylish, if brash sort of a place to show off your latest wallet-crippling Mulberry handbag on a Saturday night. It's bright, loud and busy, although during the day and early evening it's a bit more laidback. The Italian grazing menu is great for a few mates to share, or for the fat-pants with a big appetite. Their special honey cocktails, however, are a bit gloopy and sweet, and don't go so well with the food if we're honest. You're better off sticking to the champers any day. Well, you are on the Kings Road after all.

© *Mon–Thu, 12pm–12am; Fri-Sat, 12pm–2am*

⊕ *Bruschetta for 4–6 people, £15*

Sophie's Steakhouse

311–313 Fulham Road, SW10

(020) 7352 0088

⊖ Fulham Broadway

We've never met Sophie, but if she's as brawny as her food then this probably isn't the sort of place to try and pull the old dine 'n' dash. If gnawing on a huge piece of succulent cow is how you like to pass an evening, then tie that napkin round your neck and tuck in. A haven for Chelsea boys and gals with a penchant for classic cocktails, fine wines and fab food, this has established itself as the place to be when living it up out west.

© *Mon–Fri, 12pm–12am; Sat, 11am–12am; Sun, 11am–11pm*

⊕ *Black angus burger, £8.95*

❷ *£11.95*

West

KILBURN

Baker & Spice

75 Salusbury Road, Queen's Park, NW6

(020) 7604 3636

⊖ Queen's Park

This little local fave wouldn't look out of place on a Californian beachfront. With a heavy emphasis on organic food designed to keep you regular, you shouldn't go expecting a miracle hangover cure. They'll probably just tell you you shouldn't have got so drunk in the first place. That said, there's a menu of scrummy salads, mouth-watering meats and roasted vegetables, making it perfect for a healthy lunch.

⊛ *Mon–Fri, 7am–8pm; Sat, 7am–7pm; Sun, 8.30am–5pm*

⊕ *Organic lamb burger, £7.25*

Czech and Slovak House

74 West End Lane, NW6

(020) 7372 1193

⊖ West Hampstead

London's only Czech restaurant and bar, although relatively hidden on a residential street, is always heaving. There's a whiff of excitement about entering – think thick red curtains, chandeliers and the smell of spicy meat. But settle in at one of the tables and it's almost like your mate's weird gran has invited you for dinner. We'd never heard of half of what was on the menu but it all looked mighty good on everyone's plates. If you take our advice, you'll get down there pronto and Czech it out (sorry).

⊛ *Mon–Fri, 5pm–11pm; Sun, 12pm–10.30pm*

⊕ *Cabbage and pork, £6.75*

Small & Beautiful

351–353 Kilburn High Road, NW6

(020) 7328 2637

⊖ Kilburn

It's a bustling beauty of a find, this one, and your pissed–off wallet, still reeling from that recent splurge on your wardrobe, will breathe a sigh of relief when the bill comes over. Tiled floors and rickety furniture add to the cute, English feel and rib-eye steak at just £8.25 will force you to overlook the somewhat cramped surroundings and slowish service when the hungry punters pack in at dinner time. Have a pancake for pudding, with extra cream. You've worked hard.

⊛ *Mon–Sat, 12pm–12am; Sun, 12pm–11pm*

⊕ *Rib-eye steak, £8.25*

⊘ *£10*

SHEPHERD'S BUSH

Adam's Café

77 Askew Road, W12

(020) 8743 0572

⊖ Shepherd's Bush

A family-friendly affair, you'll be hard-pressed to get a seat without a four year-old buzzing round your ankles on weekends, but there's something about this Tunisian eaterie that beckons you in and sits you down without the aid of the smiley waitress. More a restaurant than a café, its prices are fair and square and we absolutely guzzled the generous portions of garlic sautéed prawns and homemade almond tart. Mmmm.

◉ *Mon–Fri, 7pm–11pm*

⊕ *Set dinner, one course and tea, £10.50*

Bush Bar & Grill

45a Goldhawk Road, W12

(020) 8746 2111

⊖ Goldhawk Road

Go and stand in the corner and think about what you've done. That's what Itchy wanted to tell the rude barman with his silly haircut after he ignored us for ten minutes then gave us the wrong drink. Having shrunk the restaurant to make way for a bigger bar, it's a shame that the folk they've hired to work behind it are such a pain. The food is decent enough, although overpriced.

◉ *Mon–Sat, 12pm–11pm;*

Sun, 12pm–10.30pm

⊕ *Roast saddle of lamb stuffed with spinach and pine nuts, new potatoes in rosemary jus, £14.50*

◪ *£12*

West

The Dove

19 Upper Mall, W6
(020) 8748 5405
⊖ Hammersmith

The old ones are the best, and having stood here as a coffee shop before becoming a pub, this 17th century building, in spite of its extensions, still houses all the charm that lured drinkers such as Hemingway and William Morris in days gone by. A great summer spot with a gorgeous river view, this charming little establishment even made it into the *Guinness Book of Records* for its microscopic bar back in 1989. Despite this, though, you never seem to have to wait long to get served, and the staff might even remember your name.

🄲 *Mon–Sat, 11am–11pm;*
Sun, 12pm–10.30pm

SOUTH KENSINGTON

Nova

312 King's Road, SW3
(020) 7351 0101
⊖ South Kensington

A sultry little basement bar that puts the champagne in the supernova and the port in Portugese. Twinkling lights adorn the low ceilings, polished punters top the high stools, and the nibbles menu sparkles with tempting-sounding titbits that upon arrival are a tad salty, not unlike miniature Findus crispy pancakes with manners; we'd skip 'em, and concentrate on the liquid offerings of the truly outstanding bar people. They're polite and dedicated, and their mixes will leave you impolite and dead. Excellent.

🄲 *Tue–Sat, 6.30pm–1am*

Ravenscourt Park Teahouse

Paddenswick Road, W6
(020) 8748 1945
⊖ Ravenscourt Park

Probably better in the summer, when the kids run amok with ice-cream on their faces and tired mothers scramble to catch the reins as they wrap themselves around the chairs. It's pure London, and once the fantastic English cooking hits your tastebuds, it'll make you proud to be British. It might be small, but the terrace offers more room in the warmer months. Try the Cumberland sausages with puy lentils. Wholesome, fresh and fabulous – like the majority of West London diners.

🄲 *Summer, Mon–Sun, 9am–dusk;*
winter, Mon–Sun, 9am–4pm
🄸 *Cumberland sausages with lentils, £7.50*

HEN PARTIES

Distinguishing features: Normally perform their all-female pre-mating ritual in a circular dance around sequined receptacles containing grooming apparel. The leader usually wears a letter L and some kind of sexual apparatus on her head.

Survival: For males under 60, camouflage is the best bet. Itchy recommends a bright pink mini-skirt, padded boob tube and red lippy.

HOMO NARCOTICUS

Distinguishing features: This unusual subspecies is mesmerised by repetitive rhythms and flashing lights, and has a peculiar ability to move all limbs and appendages at once in contrary directions, including eyes and ears.

Survival: These malcos are guaranteed to spill your drink on themselves. Put your bev in a bike bottle or go the whole way and throw a sacrificial pint at them before you start dancing.

Safe and sound

Illustration by
Thomas Denbigh

THE DANCE-FLOOR IS A SCARY REALM. IF YOU WANT TO MAKE IT OUT ALIVE, YOU'LL NEED SOME INSIDER KNOWLEDGE, SO GRAB PITH HELMET AND GLO-STICKS AND FOLLOW ITCHY ON A DISCO SAFARI

THE LADS

Distinguishing features: Alpha males indulging in competitive play, such as mixing several beverages in the same glass, and then drinking the whole lot as quickly as possible.

Survival: A propensity to punch the air during power ballads can lead to injury among taller adventurers. Itchy suggests you don a helmet and hit the deck if you hear the line 'Oooh baby do you know what that's worth?'.

UNDERAGE DRINKERS

Distinguishing features: Identified by greasy hair, pale skin and vacant eyes, this genus often regurgitate upon themselves, presenting a hazard to bystanders. Females are impervious to cold and wear very little.

Survival: Enlist their natural predators – larger and more primitive hominids called bouncers, who covet the hair of the underage drinkers, being themselves a furless species.

Gay

Gay

BARS

The Chocolate Lounge
146–148 Newington Butts, SE11
(020) 7735 5306
⊖ Kennington

How naughty. A slick and sexy members bar that's also open to friends of the LGBT community, this is probably one of the hottest places in town to hang out. It has a pool table, pole dancing, sex toy vending machine, TV lounge, dining room, chocolate fountains, and claims to be great for your hips, thighs and your love handles. With live music, drag acts and DJs, this bar/club is so cool you'll want to move in.

🕓 Tue–Thu, 5pm–12am; Fri, 7pm–2am; Sat, 7pm–4am

💷 Membership, £2 (day); £95 (annual)

The Soho Revue Bar
11 Walkers Court, W1
(020) 7734 037
⊖ Piccadilly Circus

Bang in the middle of Soho's seediest backstreets, you'd walk right past this place and on to the next sex shop if you didn't know where you were going. There's always a line of crazily dressed trannies outside and once, on the way out, we encountered not one, but two 'women' on tall stilts, trying with some difficulty to walk up the stairs. It's expensive, glitzy, glamorous fun and if you've ever wanted to curl up blissfully in a darkened corner as a gorgeous pole dancer gyrates in your general direction, Itchy's found you your new favourite place.

🕓 Times vary

Kazbar
50 Clapham High Street, SW4
(020) 7622 0070
⊖ Clapham Common

Strolling down Clapham High Street you cannot miss this corner bar for the throng of buff, well-dressed (and usually half-dressed) males complete with their compulsory pooches, spilling out onto the pavement. Quite possibly the envy of the mad plethora of Clapham watering holes – come rain or shine this place is constantly rammed. Offering up a host of special offers on shooters, pitchers and beers on a nightly basis, Kazbar makes for one riotous and hedonistic warm-up for a night in the Two Brewers club down the road.

🕓 Mon–Fri, 5pm–12am; Sat, 12pm–12am; Sun, 12pm–10.30pm

Strawberry Moons
15 Heddon Street, W1
(020) 7437 7300
⊖ Piccadilly Circus

Just about the classiest joint in town, the dress code here is black tie only, and the butlers will look askance at you if you don't order single malt. Not really. It's in tourist land, it's about as trashy as they come and we should really know better, but for picking up fresh meat, there's really no better place. People here will always buy you drinks and even if you swore you would never venture down to its murky depths, the pulse of Thursday's infamous Tribe Nights will keep forcing you to succumb and its sexy pole dancers will keep you coming back. Guilty pleasures indeed.

🕓 Times and prices vary

PUBS

The George and Dragon

2–4 Hackney Road, E2

(020) 7012 1100

⊖ Old Street/Shoreditch

This boozer is home to friendly trendies, fashion gays and a good mix of people all united by their intent to have a damn good time. It's not obviously gay at first glance, and it sometimes takes a while before folk cotton on, so take a seat by the bar and amuse yourself watching burly straights sneeze their pints out through their noses when two guys or girls start making out. Noisy but relaxed, the pub has a great jukebox and hosts a sweaty, excellent disco on Sundays.

🕒 *Mon–Sat, 12pm–11.30pm; Sun, 12pm–10.30pm*

Two Brewers

114 Clapham High Street, SW4

(020) 7498 4971

⊖ Clapham Common

So the windows are boarded up and you can never really see past the burly bouncers, but don't be deterred – once you're through the door, Brewers is one hell of a party. The 60s through to 90s disco-pop tunes, with cheap drinks, a stage and cabaret act, make for plenty of ass grinding opportunities in the front bar. The back room is a more serious deal, with shirtless punters giving it the blue steel and grooving to funky house beats among clouds of dry ice. Girls and guys alike are all just fabulous.

🕒 *Mon–Thu, 14pm–2am; Fri–Sat, 4pm–3am; Sun, 2pm–12.30am*

💷 £5

Cabaret venues

We know that snorting laughing gas from a small balloon as a girl in hotpants whizzes past on rollerblades and a woman gives birth to an egg right in front of you might not be everyone's cup of tea, but **Late Late Lunch** is one Cabaret afternoon of craziness that might just change your mind. The weirdness has been hosted by **Turnmills** (63b Clerkenwell Road, EC1, 020 7250 3409) in Farringdon during recent months, but wherever this lot lay their feathered and frilled hat feels like home. You'll never get so many wacky people in one room outside of your local mental asylum. Alternatively, if you fancy seeing some Chippendale-esque action, try **The Adonis Cabaret Show** (Club Aquarium, 256 Old Street, EC1, 0870 741 4092).

Gay

CLUES

AREA
67–68 Albert Embankment, SE11
(020) 7223 5636
⊖ Vauxhall

Here's one for more sophisticated clubbers. With live acts and cabaret on stage, it's the funky sister club of the world-famous CRASH, and consequently has most things one could ever wish for in a club, with the obvious and lamentable exception of free drinks. Head down on different nights for tribal and hard house to pop and r 'n' b, all over two big dance floors with state of the art sound and light technology, six bars and tons of room to chill out, pull and boogie.

© *Mon–Thu, 11.30pm–5am; Fri,10pm–5am; Sat, 10pm–5am; Sun, 5pm–12am*

The Pink Rupee
The Bolt Hole, 2a Suffolk Lane, EC4
(07762) 403 518
⊖ London Bridge

Saturdays will never be the same again if you're a gay Asian, or admirer of such, wondering what the hell to do on a weekend that you haven't done before. The Pink Rupee, in a relatively hidden venue near the Thames, is a mixture of Bollywood brilliance, with a sprinkling of Bhangra and one of the most exclusive (and expensive) wine lists in London. Admire from afar like a sophisticate as you sip your way through the vin rouge selection, or get up and groove like you mean it to some pop and club classics.

© *Sat, 9pm–2am*
✪ *£9/£6 concession; free before 10pm*

G-A-Y Bar
30 Old Compton Street, WC2
(020) 7494 2756
⊖ Tottenham Court Road

From the queues outside on a weekend, it doesn't take a PhD to see that this is the mother of all bars, let alone gay bars, in London. Ideally located between the tube and a host of fast food restaurants, it's easy to get to, and if you don't get your fill inside, at least you can get it on the way out. With a lesbian bar downstairs that they call 'Girls Go Down', it's one for some crazy photo opportunities, and you'd be surprised at the number of straight mates we've got who love the vibe. God bless G-A-Y, and all who sail in him/her.

© *Mon & Thu–Sat, 12pm–12am; Sun, 12pm–12am*

Trans–MISSION
The Masque Bar, 1–5 Long Lane, EC1
(07752) 945 192
⊖ Barbican

On the first Saturday of every month, London's transgendered community brings itself and its pals together for a friendly night on the tiles, which regularly attracts over 200 T-girls (transvestites, cross-dressers and transsexuals). People of all orientations are welcome to join the fabulous mixed crowd. There's dancing, drinking, chatting, laughing – you name it and it's probably going down here. If you're new to the scene however, then things can get a little confusing on occasion. When nature calls, just make sure you head for the right toilet.

© *First Sat of every month, 9pm–3am*

Gay

The Trash Palace

11 Wardour Street, W1

(020) 7734 0522

⊖ Leicester Square

At long last, a central London pub/club for those gays that don't want to wear cropped pink T-shirts while sweatily gyrating to serious, ear-shattering trance music. This small but fun-loving venue is geared towards the more discerning gent or gentress, and specialises in an excellent mix of ironic pop, indie and electro. In addition to their own decent selection of weekly nights and wallet-friendly drinks deals, they also offer queue-jump deals for Monday's Trash, Thursday's Misshapes and Friday's Popstarz. What marvellous people, we say.

© Fri–Sat, 5pm–3am; Sun–Thu, 5pm–12am

XXL London

51–53 Southwark Street, SE1

(020) 7403 4001

⊖ London Bridge

The motto of XXL is 'one club fits all', which thinking about it, isn't exactly true, but it doesn't stop the masses squeezing in on Saturday nights for a dance-a-thon in the biggest men-only club in London. You'll find the place packed with all sorts – bears, cubs, chubs and chasers, they're all getting down together here. With four rooms, two bars of art and laser shows, and two dance floors, as well as a garden area to lose the weirdo in, it don't get much better than this.

© Wed, 10pm–3am; Sat, 10pm–6am

🅐 Wed, members, free; non-members £3; Sat, members, £8; non-members £12

SO YOU'RE A FRIEND OF DOROTHY WHO'S FOUND THEMSELVES IN A NEW TOWN, AND IT MIGHT AS WELL BE THE EMERALD CITY, YOU'RE SO CLUELESSLY GREEN. HOW DO YOU TRACK DOWN THE BEST PINK PLACES? LET ITCHY GUIDE YOUR RUBY SHOES WITH SOME PEARLS OF WISDOM…

Even if their tastes aren't quite yours, they can give you the lowdown on the more subtle gay haunts, and you and Toto will be going loco in no time.

Scally or pally? – Various gay fetishes for chav-style fashions can make

Gay abandoned

There's no place like homo – Just because you're out of the closet doesn't necessarily mean that you love the great outdoors; camping it up isn't for everyone. However, the most kitsch, flamboyant venues are generally well advertised and typically the easiest ones to find; their mass appeal means you usually get a fair old proportion of straights in there too, enjoying their recommended weekly allowance of cheese, but you should have no trouble tracking down a few native chatty scenesters.

it hard to tell a friendly bear pit from a threatening lions' den full of scallies, especially if you've only heard rumours that somewhere is a non-hetters' hot spot. Be cautious in places packed with trackies unless you want your Adid-ass kicked.

Get board – Internet message boards have honest, frequently updated tips; magazines like *Diva* and *Gay Times* have links to local forums on their sites. Click your mouse, not your heels, and get ready to go on a bender.

Illustration by Si Clark
www.si-clark.co.uk

Shop

Shop

UNISEX CLOTHING

Laden Showrooms

103 Brick Lane, E1

(020) 7247 2431

⊖ Shoreditch

After some one-of-a-kind, cutting-edge fashion? Check out this gem of a boutique down Brick Lane. Founded in 1999 with a view to nurturing new talent, designers rent low-cost spaces to display and sell their products without being tied to a contract. Frequented by celebs, this treasure-trove showcases more than 45 independent designers and features a diverse range of original womenswear, menswear and accessories. It's not cheap, but it is unique.

🕒 *Mon, 12pm–6pm; Tue–Sat, 11am–6.30pm; Sun, 10.30am–6pm*

WOMEN'S CLOTHING

Labour of Love

193 Upper Street, N1

(020) 7354 9333

⊖ Angel/Highbury & Islington

Sorry, UB40 fans. This is nothing to do with Ali Campbell and co's tuneless cod reggae. Despite its location at the arse-end of Upper Street, Labour of Love has an eclectic mix of ladies' clothing, accessories, books and shoes. Quirky labels like Peter Jensen and Aganovich & Jung sit alongside DFA albums and bohemian lifestyle books. Not cheap, but good for brownie-point presents. Unless they're after *Rat In Me Kitchen* on vinyl, in which case you're best off without 'em.

🕒 *Mon–Sat, 10.30am–6.30pm; Sun, 12.30pm–5.30pm*

nothingshop

230 Portobello Road, W11

(020) 7221 2910

⊖ Notting Hill Gate

They say that when you're in Rome you should do as the Romans do (although doesn't that mean spending yer hols vomiting during meals?). Which means that when you're in this joint you should sure as hell make sure that you ignore the staff because they're sure as hell gonna ignore you. If you're just an ordinary browser with no dosh on display, forget getting any kind of service in this place. In spite of its carefully selected designer trends (Soochi, Gsus, Jenny Hellstrom and T Cuff etc), the nothingshop is strictly there for if there's absolutely nothing to see in the market.

🕒 *Mon–Sat, 11am–6pm*

SECONDHAND

Bang Bang

9 Berwick Street, W1

(020) 7631 4191

⊖ **Piccadilly Circus**

'Bang bang, you're dead', sang Dirty Pretty Things. Little did they know this place would be doing so well not long after. This ladies' and gents' clothing exchange stocks secondhand high-street, vintage and designer clothing. Despite the small size of the shop, there is something for everyone, from a high-street top at £5 to a £300 McQueen showstopper, and a plethora of excellent vintage for both sexes. They also buy off the public, so it's one to remember for those skint end-of-the-month moments.

☺ *Mon–Sat, 10.30am–7pm*

Collectors Centre

Wood Street Market,

98 Wood Street, E17

(020) 8520 4032

⊖ **Walthamstow Central**

On a list of classic things to do in Walthamstow, its rare for most guides to mention the 'Stow's most hidden gem and prized asset. But Itchy isn't your average guide. Much more interesting than its famous high-street counterparts, Wood Street Market is a nostalgia collectors wet dream. From vintage second hand records and toys from the 50s and 60s to film and TV memorabilia and the best secondhand bookshop this side of East London, it's worth schlepping down here just to inhale the dust in this little time bubble. Old Lahndan tahn at its best.

☺ *Mon–Fri, 10am–5.30pm*

Exclusivo

24 Hampstead High Street, NW3

(020) 7431 8618

⊖ **Hampstead**

Exclusivo's crammed full of more second-hand designer items than Laurence Llewelyn-Bowen's wardrobe. It's a bit poky though, so you'll have to hunt hard to find the right item in this often overlooked Hampstead store, but you won't regret seeking it out for its fabulous discount shoe collection, designer clothing at about half the original price and the occasional new collection samples from current designers. Impossible to navigate when busy, but quite exciting when there's space to move around and trawl through piles of crap to find the good Gucci and Chanel stuff underneath.

☺ *Mon–Sat, 11.30am–6pm*

Shop

Rellik

8 Golborne Road, W10

(020) 8962 0089

⊖ Westbourne Park

A vintage emporium and a must for fashion devotees far and wide. Rellik may be a tad pricier than the nearby market stalls, but if you're looking for bona fide designer vintage this store will be your bag, baby. Whether it's belts, berets, bags, brooches, boots or braces, the clothes rails are crammed with achingly fabulous pieces by Westwood, Dior, Biba, Ossie Clark and Pucci to name but a few. There's an outstanding selection of eclectic vintage couture, the staff really know their stuff, and are on hand to give you honest and sound advice on your potential period purchases.

◉ *Tue–Sat, 10am–6pm*

Rokit

101–107 Brick Lane, E1

(020) 7375 3864

⊖ Shoreditch/Aldgate East

Haunt of the funky, monied East End trendies, this rather pricey store carries an interesting and quirky selection of vintage, second-hand, customised and own-designed items from ball gowns and jeans to bags, shoes, jewellery and other fun accessories – some are fabulous, some hideous, and it has a particularly large cowboy boot collection. You can probably find cheaper vintage items elsewhere (especially if you happen to catch a rag and bone man), but if you're in the area this is worth a look, along with the nearby Absolute Vintage and Beyond Retro.

◉ *Mon–Fri, 11am–7pm; Sat–Sun, 10am–7pm*

BOOKS

Foyles

113–119 Charing Cross Road, WC2

(020) 7437 5660

⊖ Tottenham Court Road

It's hard to believe that anything bad could ever happen to you in Foyles. One of London's oldest bookstores, the Charing Cross Road mammoth has oodles of choice spread over its six floors. You'll find weighty art tomes nestled next to travel guides, or Godard film criticism stuck by the novelty fart-joke books. As well as all this, it has a funky jazz and soul record store on the first floor, next to a lovely café which serves the best damn carrot cake in the whole of town. Check it out.

◉ *Mon–Sat, 9.30am–9pm; Sun, 12pm–6pm*

Gosh!

39 Great Russell Street, WC1
(020) 7636 1011

⊖ Tottenham Court Road

Let's get one thing straight, you don't have to be a certified comic book geek to admire the selection of great stuff in this little jewel: from classic children's picture books to graphic novels, to the latest *X-Men* comic. Whether you're checking out the latest Alan Moore or want to introduce your nephew to the delights of the Silver Surfer, any self-respecting escapist walking through Bloomsbury should pop in here for a look... just don't let anyone see you. Comics might not be just for kids, but most people have a funny way of assuming they are.

🕒 *Mon–Wed, 10am–6pm; Thu–Fri, 10am–7pm; Sat, 10am–6pm*

Blackwell's

100 Charing Cross Road, WC2
(020) 7292 5100

⊖ Tottenham Court Road

So much more than just a bookshop, this place has everything. Well, it's got books, CDs, DVDs and cards. And some posters and calendars. And novelty bookmarks.

🕒 *Mon–Sat, 9.30am–8pm; Sun, 12pm–6pm*

Books Etc

66 Victoria Street, SW1
(020) 7931 0677

⊖ Victoria

Books do feature here, despite a name that suggests a cavalier disregard for them. Imagine how the stuff termed 'Etc' feels.

🕒 *Mon–Fri, 8.30am–7pm; Sat, 9.30am–6pm; Sun, 12pm–6pm*

Grant and Cutler

55–57 Great Marlborough Street, W1
(020) 7734 2012

⊖ Oxford Circus

If you want to expand your foreign patter past Cockney rhyming slang, (which you should do really, seeing as you're in the greatest cosmopolitan city on earth), then this is the place to come. G&C is the best foreign language bookseller in town by far, packed from top to toe with an incredible selection covering over 200 languages. From ancient Greek to Gaelic, its all here. Although if any of you encounter a part of London where people actually converse in ancient Greek, we'd love to hear from you.

🕒 *Mon–Wed, 9am–6pm, Thu–Fri, 9am–7pm; Sat, 9am–5pm; Sun, 12pm–6pm*

Borders

203 Oxford Street, W1
(020) 7292 1600

⊖ Oxford Circus

What with the skin-crawlingly efficient 20Q game that can read your mind, you may not even have time to read all the cards in Paperchase, let alone pick up a book.

🕒 *Mon–Sat, 8am–11pm; Sun, 12pm–6pm*

Waterstone's

82 Gower Street, WC1
(020) 7636 1577

⊖ Goodge Street

Not for us the flagship Piccadilly store, oh no. We infinitely prefer the cosier, academic feel of UCL's smaller local.

🕒 *Mon–Fri, 9.30am–8pm; Sat, 9.30am–7pm; Sun, 12pm–6pm*

Shop

Keith Fawkes Book Shop

1–3 Flask Walk, Hampstead, NW3

(020) 7435 0614

⊖ Hampstead

Cosily tucked down a pedestrian side street, this small but well-stocked secondhand bookshop is haphazardly packed to the ceilings with an impressive collection of fiction and non-fiction at bargain prices. From classics, philosophy and modern fiction to travel books, the friendly and helpful staff can usually point you in the right direction amidst the confusion. Even if you don't know what you want, it's still a good place to partake in a leisurely afternoon's browse among the musty shelves and faint smell of pipe tobacco.

🕒 *Mon–Fri, 10am–5.30pm; Sun, 12pm–6pm*

MUSIC

Fopp

220–224 Tottenham Court Road, W1

(020) 7299 1640

⊖ Goodge Street

The chain's new, huge store on Tottenham Court Road is situated in the old Purves & Purves building. It contains a genius mix of £3 nasties – David Hasselhoff sings smooth classics, anyone? – with decently priced indie releases and £5 versions of all the classics that ought to be in any right-thinking person's record collection. The shop's confusing categorisation of CDs is tempered by the huge basement bar serving cheap food and, more brilliantly, booze. A perfect way to spend an afternoon.

🕒 *Mon–Sat, 10am–10pm; Sun, 12pm–6pm*

Magma

117–119 Clerkenwell Road, EC1

(020) 7242 9503

⊖ Chancery Lane

Indulge your inner geek with Magma's brilliant selection of film and music magazines, fanzines, odd T-shirts and cartoon statuettes.

🕒 *Mon–Sat, 10.30am–6.30pm;*

Sun, 12.30pm–5.30pm

WH Smith

The Plaza, 120 Oxford Street, W1

(020) 7436 6282

⊖ Oxford Circus

Is it a bookshop? A stationer's? A sweetshop? It's whatever you want. Grab the wine gums and Mills and Boon and stop the questions.

🕒 *Mon–Wed & Fri–Sat, 10am–7pm;*

Thu, 10am–8pm; Sun, 12pm–6pm

Intoxica!

231 Portobello Road, W11

(020) 7229 8010

⊖ Ladbroke Grove

London's answer to the shop in *High Fidelity* – if you're in search of that collector's German export edition of a rare Beatles LP, you're bound to find it here. Offering a host of second-hand collectable LPs & 45s, from £10 to £600, Intoxica! stocks an eclectic mix of specialist vinyl ranging from 50s rock 'n' roll, 60s soul, 70s funk and 80s & 90s pop, to jazz, surf, latin, reggae and ska. The owners seriously know their vinyl, and if they don't stock what you're after, they'll do their utmost to order it in for you. They even stock rare film posters, often in foreign languages, selling for about £30–£80.

🕒 *Mon–Sat, 10.30am–6.30pm; Sun, 12pm–5pm*

HMV

150 Oxford Street, W1

(020) 7631 3423

⊖ **Oxford Circus**

Hum Music Vocally. That's what we believe 'HMV' stands for, and we obey this to the letter when plugged in at the listening posts.

🕒 **Mon–Wed & Fri–Sat, 9am–8.30pm; Thu, 9am–9pm; Sun, 12pm–6pm**

Virgin Megastore

14–19 Oxford Street

(020) 7631 1234

⊖ **Oxford Circus**

You may feel like a corporate whore for shopping here, but there are some days when all you want to do is froth at the mouth in a haze of spend, spend, spending.

🕒 **Mon–Sat, 9.30am–9pm; Sun, 12pm–6pm**

FOOD

Planet Organic

42 Westbourne Grove, W2

(020) 7221 7171

⊖ **Bayswater**

Fresh, fresh and even fresher, this organic supermarket brings a little bit of the country to London Town. With two more stores in Fulham and Torrington Place, plus a home delivery service, it won't be long before the whole city is feasting on hampers of GM-free foodstuffs. It's slightly out of the way from all the other supermarkets but is well worth the trek just to sample the yummy freebies. However, the staff do sometimes have a tendency to get up their own arses. Which is rich considering that they're mostly patchouli-smoking hippies.

🕒 **Mon–Sat, 9am–8pm; Sun, 11am–5pm**

The Spice Shop

1 Blenheim Crescent, W11

(020) 7221 4448

⊖ **Ladbroke Grove**

A curry addict's dream. Homegrown from a mere market stall set up in 1990 on Portobello Road, The Spice Shop is now situated in petite premises just off the famous market street. The grotto-like interior's adorned with tins and bags of rich smelling herbs and spices, and offers a colossal range of 2,500 products. This mini spice palace is one of a kind in the UK and now attracts famous TV chefs who come to gather inspiration from their self-made recipes. Tip: try the raz el hanout spice at £2.55 per bag – every seed they stock goes into making this spice. May your dishes never be dull again.

🕒 **Mon–Sat, 9.30am–6pm; Sun, 10am–4pm**

Shop

OTHER

Bean Bag Shop

Stables Market, NW1
(020) 7482 0444
⊖ **Chalk Farm**

Conveniently located in food and drink spiller's paradise, the comfy bean bags that litter the area around this stall are frequently squished into the shapes of punks, rockers, shoppers and drunks. Too good to pass by without flopping into for a little bit, the guys here must rake in a fortune. You know you want one in your living room, and why not when prices start from just £29 for a small one, right up to £99 for a sofa-sized version.

🕒 *Mon–Fri, 10am–5pm;*
Sat–Sun, 10am–6pm

James Smith and Son

53 New Oxford Street, WC1
(020) 7836 4731
⊖ **Tottenham Court Road**

We live in London. It rains. But don't settle for one of the boring black umbrellas that crowd the miserable streets. You want the very best if you're going to stand out. So head to James Smith, who've been doling out brollies of every description on the same spot for 179 years. One is free to wander and browse without any grief from the staff; even a relative peasant like Itchy was left well alone. They also sell canes, flasks and other Victorian-style paraphernalia, so you can leave here feeling like the epitome of the old-fashioned aristo.

🕒 *Mon–Fri, 9.30am–5.25pm;*
Sat, 10am–5.25pm

Gash

www.gash.co.uk

When Itchy's mate Dave discovered this über-classy online erotic emporium, stocking lingerie, cosmetics, books, lotions, and lady-pleasing toys including the 'Tongue Joy', he declared, 'That's just like the rhyming kitchen product: Gash – loves the jobs you hate'. This revealed both his dire bedroom prowess and an acute lack of grease-busting knowledge – that's Mr Muscle, not Flash, twazzock. When he's finished with the sink, we've got his girlie some personalised pants to help him patch things up, emblazoned with a photo of his mug and the words 'Dave, come on down'. Our own de-luxe satin pair look stunning, but maybe having them embroidered with 'Itchy' wasn't such a good idea.

Oddballs

Camden Lock Market, Chalk Farm Road, NW1
(020) 7284 4488
⊖ **Camden Town**

It might just be a load of old balls to some people, but for the serious jugglers among us, this Camden classic, open for an impressive 22 years, is the dog's danglies. Boasting the largest range of juggling equipment in the country (which, thankfully, has absolutely nothing to do with dogs' bollocks) and backed up by an online store with even more stock for all your circus needs, this one-stop freak shop is even run by jugglers, so pop in for a quick display of how to really go about handling a good pair of balls.

🕒 *Mon–Fri, 10am–5pm;*
Sat–Sun, 10am–6pm

IF YOU THINK VEGGIES ARE CRANKY, YOU'LL LOVE THIS. FREEGANS SAY OUR ECONOMIC SYSTEM HURTS THE ENVIRONMENT, TREATS ANIMALS CRUELLY AND WORKERS UNFAIRLY, AND WASTES RESOURCES, SO YOU SHOULDN'T PAY FOR FOOD. IDIOTS. HERE'S HOW WE'D BE FREEGANS…

1. Have a Pret dinner – The bods who run Pret a Manger obviously don't know much about the principles of Freeganism, given how much they throw away each day. Turn up at closing, rummage through their bin bags, and hey presto – free dinner.

2. Kill an animal – Apparently it's legal for you to kill squirrels on your own property. With this in mind, set up a bird table, cover it in superglue and get the pot boiling while you wait for it to become a squirrel lolly. Sure, you might snare the odd bird, but extra protein's always welcome, and the RSPB'll never catch you.

3. Forage – Those in the country could nick apples from trees and scour woodland floors for wild mushrooms. Alternatively, those of us whose parents aren't blood-related to each other could pull half-eaten trays of late-night chips from bins.

4. Mug a milkman – Those bastards don't need all that milk. But you do. Being a freegan isn't conducive to a calcium-rich diet, after all. Wait until your local milky's delivering to a dark area, then knock him out and chug as many bottles as you can before making your getaway.

5. Sniper rifle the zoo – Get up high, and train your gun on the elephant cage. It's not going to be easy to take one of those suckers down with one shot, but if it pays off, you'll be eating like a monarch for weeks. Plus you could sell the tusks on to practitioners of Chinese medicine for extra cash.

Freegan fun

Illustration by Thomas Denbigh

0800700200
FREE
PHONE

G.A.N
SKIP HIRE

8 BOWLING LANES

Basement of Tavistock Hotel, Bedford Way, off Russell Square, London, WC1

LIVE BANDS

COCKTAIL BAR

DINER

PRIVATE KARAOKE ROOMS

OPEN TIL 3AM

www.bloomsburybowling.com
bookings@bloomsburybowling.com
Tel: 020 7 691 2610   Bookings: 020 7 168 9616

Out & about

Out & about

CINEMAS

Clapham Picture House

76 Venn Street, SW4

(08707) 550 061

⊖ Clapham Common

Another cosy cinema, complete with its own café and fortnightly film quiz, the Picture House is also conveniently close to Clapham's nightlife and numerous restaurants which is very handy if you're planning on taking things further once the film's over. Its local feel and backstreet location also make sitting through a film seem a little less clinical than if you went to a larger venue – Itchy thoroughly recommends the place for a lazy Sunday afternoon flick.

🎬 *Times and prices vary*

The Electric Brasserie

191 Portobello Road, W11

(020) 7908 9696

⊖ Notting Hill Gate

The first time we read this place's name, we thought it was called 'The Electric Brassiere'. An interesting concept, but possibly a bit 'specialist'. This cosy West London picture house is an Itchy favourite, and compared to your run-of-the-mill high street chain cinema it's The Savoy to Alan Partridge's Travel Tavern. Couples can get themselves comfy on the cuddle chairs and you get a proper table for food rather than a bucket and a plastic hole in your seat. Oh and the films are usually pretty good too – a mix of decent Hollywood flicks and some rarer pieces.

🎬 *Times and prices vary*

Curzon Mayfair

38 Curzon Street, W1

(020) 7495 0500

⊖ Green Park

Probably the poshest cinema Itchy has ever been to, they serve the popcorn in gold-plated boxes and you can get bottles of Moët brought to your seat just by clapping your hands. So that's not quite true, but it should be – it would make the fine selection of cinematic rarities and international film even more interesting. Take a date here and he/she will think you're a sophisticated, cultured film lover as long as you don't pick *American Pie 5* as the evening's movie. If Mayfair's a bit far out then check London's other Curzon in Soho. It's on Shaftesbury Avenue.

🎬 *Times and prices vary*

Odeon Leicester Square

Leicester Square, WC2

(08712) 244 007

⊖ Leicester Square

Yeah we know it's a big old chain cinema, but if we're going to review one of then it really might as well be this place. After all, we reckon it merits it. The leopard print seats have been warmed by countless celebs at glitzy premieres and a decade of BAFTAs ('til they moved to the Opera House). Because of this and the cinema's prime location (doesn't come much more central and film-orientated than slap-bang on Leicester Square), it isn't cheap but they do show a lot of big films days before the official release date. And there's nothing like seeing a film before all your mates have.

🎬 *Times and prices vary*

Pub quizzes

The Roxy

3 Rathbone Place, W1

⊖ Tottenham Court Road

(020) 7255 1098

This late-night Soho spot degenerates into a puke-worthy crush of indie kids past 10.30pm, but the monthly Airport pop quiz offers tons of cool prizes like T-shirts and CDs. Turn up early for a seat and bribe the brainiacs with some of the bargain beers available.

First Mon of every month, 8pm, £1

The Boogaloo

312 Archway Road, N6

⊖ Highgate

(020) 8340 2928

We love the multimedia extravaganza of the 'You're Gonna Need a Bigger Boat' film quiz. Think photos, tunes, posters and lots of giggles – the Boogaloo is always full of really friendly people. Aaaw. With no limit on team sizes and lovely film-related prizes this is a true Itchy fave.

First Wed of every month, 8.30pm, £1

The Oxford Arms

265 Camden High Street, NW1

⊖ Camden Town

(020) 7267 4945

This quiz has been running for ten years and draws the Camden crowds with its promise of free food at the end for all participants. It's only decent to buy a few drinks, and as the prize is cold, hard cash for first, second and third place, then you can maybe buy a few more after.

Mon, 9pm, free

The Frog and Forget-me-not

204 Dawes Road, SW4

⊖ Clapham Common

(020) 7610 2598

You've got to get there by at least 7pm to bag a seat, but that's no problem when the food is the best on the block – try the Thai green curry and weep. This squishy-sofa haven is a fave for Commoners but people travel from afar for this free pop quiz. Well worth it for a mid-week mingle.

Tue, 8.30pm, free

Out & about

The Rio Cinema

103 Kingsland High Street, E8
(020) 7241 9410
⊖ Dalston Kingsland (BR)

A genuine East End cinema, the Rio has an excellent reputation for being a nice place to watch a film, (which is probably a good job for a cinema really – though it wouldn't be so great if it was, say, a barber's, or a plumbing shop), plus it plays host to some unusual flicks alongside the more mainstream selection. The Rio has also hosted the Kurdish Film Festval, so maybe Kazakhstan will get in on the act to try and trump Borat in 2007? Drinks and popcorn are well priced, which is handy if you go and see films like the recent four hour-long Andy Warhol documentary.

🎬 *Times and prices vary*

The Ritzy Cinema

Brixton Oval, Coldharbour Lane, SW2
(08707) 550 062
⊖ Brixton

Situated in the heart of vibrant Brixton, The Ritzy is a South London favourite, partly on account of its refreshing balance between mainstream and independent film programming, as well as its on-site café with free wifi access. If you've got the little nephews and nieces staying for the weekend and they've tired of standing in beer gardens with an Appletiser while you 'quickly talk grown-up things to a man inside', then regular family screenings and Saturday matinees for kids are popular, and it's a Danny DeVito-sized walk from the tube to the cinema.

🎬 *Times and prices vary*

Giggy bank

FORGET ALL THAT RUBBISH ABOUT THE NORTHERN MUSIC SCENE, LONDON IS AND ALWAYS HAS BEEN THE HOME OF ROCK 'N' ROLL IN THE UK. HERE'S WHERE TO TAKE IN SOME OF ITS BETTER OFFERINGS

Bloomsbury Bowling

Basement of the Tavistock Hotel, Bedford Way, off Russell Square, WC1

(020) 7691 2610

⊖ **Goodge Street**

If your appreciation of gigs generally involves handling balls, we'd suggest you stick to more 'specialist' venues. However, this ace 50s-style bowling alley's roster of acts from Thursday to Saturday means you can get a hold of a couple of round ones as you listen, with no gimp mask required.

The Borderline

Orange Yard, off Manette Street, W1

(020) 7534 6970

⊖ **Tottenham Court Road**

For slightly newer bands than you might see at the Academy, check out the Borderline in Soho. As you walk down the stairs you'll see the impressive list of bands who have appeared over the venue's long history. There's a good chance that the band playing that evening are on the road to world domination, too.

93 Feet East

150 Brick Lane, E1

(020) 7247 3293

⊖ **Shoreditch/Liverpool Street**

Situated in the heart of curry and club land, 93FE's where Nathan Barley would go for a cheeky beer after work and maybe dance badly to cutting-edge electronica after a few too many. Joking aside, this is an Itchy fave for late night dancing and boozing to some excellent bands, and the courtyard is great in the summer.

Barfly

49 Chalk Farm Road, NW1

(020) 7691 4244

⊖ **Chalk Farm**

Not only has the Barfly given birth to many of the capital's best bands, but its club nights are legendary too, specifically the bi-weekly Casino Royale. All the beer is served in plastic glasses which only adds to the strangely dingy students' union atmosphere. As do all the oddly-dressed peeps that look like art students.

Out & about

OUTDOOR SWIMMING

Brockwell Park Lido
Dulwich Road, SE24
(020) 7274 3088
⊖ Brixton

Opened all the way back in 1937, this enormous concrete hole is a staple for South Londoners and one of the most famous lidos in the big smoke. This is the place to chill out in the months when it's warming up, and you can even take a meditation class if the soothing melodies of everyday Lambeth life are doing your head in. Speaking for ourselves, Itchy infinitely prefers the screech of traffic to Atlantic whale song, but each to their own, as our gran used to say.
◐ *Times and prices vary*

Hornsey Park Road Lido
Park Road, N8
(020) 8341 3567
⊖ Hornsey (BR)

Open all year round, we have on occasion wondered what sort of masochistic nut job thinks it's an appealing idea to fling themselves in freezing water in the middle of January. Probably the same sort of person who puts TCP on shaving cuts. Thinking about it, they might be on to something in that, come summer, you're going to have to dodge a lot of chavs if you want a swim, but then again grassy verges and a fun fountain that doesn't just have to be for the kids (ahem) make for a day of hot, wet fun outside the bedroom. Well, it's something different…
◐ *Times and prices vary*

Hampton Heated Open Air Pool
Hampton, Twickenham, TW12
(020) 8979 9933
⊖ Hampton (BR)

It's recently refurbished, so you probably won't find any little presents from the local canines, empty fag packets or used connies floating around with your stray armbands any more. Which is always nice. A refreshing summer dip here is proper swimming in a glorious and historic spot. It's London lounging at its best, and great for checking out a bit of that tasty Twickenham totty. Just don't come here after you've been playing rugby. You might get blood in the pool, and the dogs will smell it. It's all downhill from there.
◐ *Times and prices vary*

Oasis Swimming Pool
32 Endell Street, WC2
(020) 8940 0561
⊖ Tottenham Court Road

For when you really fancy having a splash about. Definitely… maybe. They don't have any water slides, which is sad, because if they did, you could slide away. Perhaps the most cosmopolitan of inner-city swimming pools, this Manc-inspired lido is popular among the workers. Pretend to be drowning, then when the lifeguard comes running, sing 'cos maybeeeee, yer gonna be the one that saves meeeee'. Go in the summer so you can lounge in the sun-shee-ayne, and don't rush off too fast, or your mates will ask 'where were you while we were getting dry?'
◐ *Times and prices vary*

Park life

IT'S GOT NOTHING TO DO WITH YOUR VORSPRUNG DURCH TECHNIK YOU KNOW. OH NO, IT'S ABOUT NOT PAYING FOR DECKCHAIRS OR FESTIVALS

Richmond Park
Bog Lodge Yard, TW10
⊖ Richmond

Richmond's not long been named the most desirable spot to live in London, and when you step off the train among leafy trees of green you can easily see why. You might get trampled by a deer, but we're just glad of a place nearby that still has any form of wildlife. After all, we need to eat. Not that we're suggesting you go down with a tranquiliser gun...

Victoria Park
Approach Road, E2
⊖ Bethnal Green

Victoria Park plays host to London's best fireworks display in November, but in the summer the families flock from all around to lounge around by the giant lake and feed the ducks. With a bandstand and ice-cream stops a-plenty, it's like living in a real life scene from Mary Poppins. Supercalafragi... well, you know what we mean.

St James's Park
Central London, SW1
⊖ St James's Park

Close to Buckingham Palace, this patch of greenery is awash with tourists and office workers alike in summer. The lakes are beautiful and you can't get more romantic than strolling round here with your loverboy/girl. Meet for a sneaky lunch break beneath a tree, but don't get caught sitting on a deckchair unless you've paid. You'll get a slapped wrist.

Clapham Common
South West London, SW4–11
⊖ Clapham Common

You can hardly move without getting hit by a flying football on summer weekends, but that's the price you have to pay for eyeing up the shirtless Aussies who seem to make up as much of the lawn as the grass. With festivals galore in July and August it's the spot for a picnic, whether you're paying or not. Hey, music travels...

Out & about

THEATRES

London Palladium

Argyll Street, W1
(020) 7637 9041
⊖ **Oxford Circus**

With 2,286 seats, the Palladium is one of London's biggest theatres, but to be honest we wouldn't recommend you bag a seat at the top. Exciting it may be, but if you suffer from even the mildest of vertigo, you're not going to be doing yourselves any favours. As host to the Royal Variety Performance since 1914 there's always a queue to whatever top show manages to open inside – most recently *Chitty Chitty Bang Bang* gave way to the digital, laser spectacular *Sinatra*.
Ⓒ *Times and prices vary*

The Roundhouse

Chalk Farm Road, NW1
(020) 7424 9991
⊖ **Chalk Farm**

Originally built as a railway shed in 1846, the Roundhouse has long since been known as a top London arts venue, and throughout the 60s and 70s a ton of top acts performed here, including Jimi Hendrix, Pink Floyd, Peter Brook and The Living Theatre of New York. In recent years it had started to become a little bit of a sad shadow of its former self in a lot of ways, but since its extensive refurbishment you can now catch some top music acts as well as weird, arty performances, and don't miss a drink on the splendid roof terrace in the summer.
Ⓒ *Times and prices vary*

National Theatre

South Bank, SE1
(020) 7452 3000
⊖ **Waterloo**

This Thames-side beauty spot used to be a barren wasteland that became a rather good place to go sleep in old fish and chip wrappers or smoke a contemplative crack pipe or two as the sun went down. But regeneration means that now the South Bank is a bustling, trendy place to hang, with a host of brand new eateries to lure you in. Among all this new-found glory, the National stands proud, lighting up the waterfront with a purple glow. Don't miss the £10 sponsored tickets to some of the best theatre and art performances in the country.
Ⓒ *Times and prices vary*

Comedy

WHAT'S BROWN AND STICKY? A STICK. OH ALRIGHT,
SO OUR STAND-UP MIGHT NEED A LITTLE WORK.
TRY ONE OF THESE FOR A BIT MORE OF A BELLY LAUGH

THE ALBANY

240 Great Portland Street, W1

(020) 7387 5706

www.lowdownatthealbany.com

⊖ Great Portland Street

Downstairs at The Albany is a comedy goldmine. Not only is it home to regular evenings of humour, but the tiny venue means you may well end up part of the gag. We've been variously accused of having crow's eyes, looking like a fat child and being a stalker, but each time it was so hilarious we couldn't make ourselves care.

THE COMEDY PUB

7 Oxendon Street, SW1

(020) 7839 7261

⊖ Piccadilly Circus

In the heart of the West End, The Comedy Pub puts on well-known comedians and doesn't generally tend to close 'til 2am. As well as their upstairs gig, there's the Big Night Out Comedy Club in the basement, which hosts several top comedy nights, including Itchy fave The Runaway Lovers on Sundays – a slice of comic genius from four men and a lady.

THE KING'S HEAD

2 Crouch End Hill, N8

(020) 8340 1028

www.downstairsatthekingshead.com

⊖ Finsbury Park

If you fancy a trip to leafy Crouch End, home of the muesli-eating chattering classes, then check out North London's best comedy venue, The King's Head. Their ace entertainment ranges from a story-telling contest (the bigger the lie the better…) to Sunday afternoon jazz. Just don't forget a copy of *The Guardian* if you want to fit in.

THE BEDFORD

77 Bedford Hill, SW12

(020) 8682 8940

www.thebedford.co.uk

⊖ Balham

Friday and Saturday's weekly Banana Cabaret night has been going for over 20 years. It's a bit pricey, especially when you compare it to the more central clubs and their handy locations, but the spacious bar, late licence and nearby rail and bus links mean you can laugh your arse off and then stagger home when you're ready.

Out & about

MUSICALS

Cabaret
Lyric Theatre, Shaftesbury Avenue, W1
(020) 7494 5045
⊖ Piccadilly Circus

Not the best show in town, but if you want something sexy and dark, head to the Kit Kat Club. Ps. Full frontal is on the menu. So don't take your gran.

Dirty Dancing
The Aldwych Theatre, Aldwych, WC2
(020) 7379 3367
⊖ Holborn

'I carried a watermelon'. Well it had to start somewhere. When Baby met Johnny is the basis of our all time fave 80s movie, and they've left no tutu unturned in this version.

Spamalot
The Palace Theatre, Cambridge Circus, W1
(020) 7434 0909
⊖ Leicester Square

It's a deliberate rip-off of *The Holy Grail,* but if you loved that film you'll wet your pants over this. Eric Idle's score features a whole heap of brand new songs, still, 'look on the bright side' – all the old faves are there.

Wicked
Apollo Victoria Theatre, Wilton Road, SW1
(020) 7834 6318
⊖ Victoria

If an all singing, all dancing, over the rainbow spectacular is what your heart desires, this award winning smash hit will get your ruby slipper-clad toes a-tap-tap-tapping. And yes, there are munchkins. Lots of them.

Fest for success

Clapham Common

www.claphamcommon.org

⊖ Clapham Common

Hosts a number of small festivals during the summer, covering everything from extreme sports to ice cream. Most have live music and food stalls, but if you stick around past the end, don't be surprised to find some friendly strangers wandering round. This is Clapham Common, after all.

☎ *See local press for event details over the summer*

City of London Festival

Various venues in Central London

(08451) 207 502

www.colf.org

The City of London Festival is a bit more upmarket and is held annually across June and July in the Square Mile. Highbrow culture such as pottery exhibitions and art installations are the order of the day, so make sure you plan something interesting for the evening.

☎ *See website for event details*

London Film Festival

Various venues in Central London

(020) 7928 3232

www.lff.org.uk

Held during October and November, the world-renowned London Film Festival is a must for any cinephile and covers dozens of events including debates and screenings. Itchy hopes they show that obscure, vaguely obscene Swedish documentary about nudism in 1960s Scandinavia again.

Chinese New Year

Various venues in and around W1

18th February 2007/2nd July 2008

⊖ Leicester Square

Chinese New Year is one of London's noisiest and most lively street festivals. It's scheduled for 18th February in 2007, but leave the dog at home – the bangers and chefs' cleavers will terrify them. Also, don't expect to get anywhere in a hurry, as the streets get totally rammed.

☎ *See local press for details*

Out & about

GALLERIES

Hayward Gallery

South Bank Centre, Belvedere Road, SE1

(020) 7921 0813

⊖ Waterloo

Sitting on the south bank of the Thames, between the National Theatre and the Royal Festival Hall, it makes a great stop on your tour of all things arty. It was opened by the Queen in 1968 and remains a bit of an icon of sixties brutalist architecture. The colours in the big neon tower, currently being refurbished, are activated by changes in the strength and direction of the wind. But no, blowing on it won't help.

🕒 *Mon, Thu & Sat–Sun, 10am–6pm; Tue–Wed, 10am–8pm; Fri, 10am–9pm*

💷 *£5*

ICA

The Mall, SW1

(020) 7930 3647

⊖ Charing Cross

Otherwise known as The Institute of Contemporary Art, this bustling spot has become as much of a cool place to hang out and talk about important modern day issues as the place to find the best up and coming talent in the art-world. Showing films and exhibitions, and offering a bar with pumping DJ and funky crowd, this one's an obvious choice for your visiting mates to find out why you moved to 'cultural' London. (Ahem).

🕒 *Mon, 12pm–11pm; Tue–Sat, 12pm–1am; Sun, 12pm–10.30pm*

💷 *Mon–Fri, £2/£1.50 concs; Sat–Sun, £3/£2 concs*

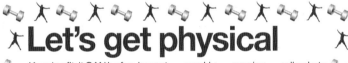

Let's get physical

Keeping fit: it CAN be fun, honest. Improve both your fitness and stripping technique at the same time with a burlesque class at the **Bethnal Green Working Men's Club** (44–46 Pollard Row, E2, 020 7739 2727). If you can master the anti-clockwise nipple tassel rotation manoeuvre after a few lessons you'll be one step ahead of the amateurs at Itchy Towers. Or you could join the crazed loons on the weekly evening rollerskate around Central London (www.londonskate.com). If something indoors is more your thing check out Bloomsbury's super-cool **All Star Bowling Lanes** (Victoria House, Bloomsbury Place, WC1, 020 7025 2676). As well as lanes, they have karaoke rooms and host club nights, so prepare yourself for an evening of bowling, boogying, boozing and all other things that begin with 'b'.

Calling all aspiring scribblers and snappers...

We need cheeky writers and hawk-eyed photographers to contribute their sparkling talents to the Itchy city guides and websites. We want the inside track on the bars, pubs, clubs and restaurants in your city, as well as longer features and dynamic pictures to represent the comedy, art, music, theatre, cinema and sport scenes.

If you're interested in getting involved, please send examples of your writing or photography to: editor@itchymedia.co.uk, clearly stating which city you can work in. All work will be fully credited.

Bath/Birmingham/Brighton/Bristol/Cambridge/Cardiff/Edinburgh/ Glasgow/Leeds/Liverpool/London/Manchester/ Nottingham/Oxford/Sheffield/York

Out & about

Photographers' Gallery
5 & 8 Great Newport Street, WC2
(020) 7831 1772
�'t Leicester Square

So you're in that disorientating no-man's land between Covent Garden and Leicester Square, and it's pissing down with rain? Well, there are worse things you could do than huddle under this little cultural umbrella and soak up the various changing exhibitions by photographers from all over the world. With two buildings, one hosting a café and gallery, the other a bookshop and the chance to buy photos, there's plenty to keep you amused until the rain passes.

ⓒ *Mon–Wed & Fri–Sat, 11am–6pm;*
Thu, 11am–8pm; Sun, 12pm–6pm
ⓔ *Free*

The Saatchi Gallery
The Duke of York's HQ building, King's Road, SW3
www.saatchi-gallery.co.uk
➟ Sloane Square
Opening summer 2007

Having closed its South Bank doors, the masters of contemporary art are shifting to a newer, sleeker location ready for summer 2007, when they'll attract presumably just as many toffs as art-boffs on the Kings Road. A little art bird has told us the new gallery will have huge, high-ceilinged rooms, a book shop, educational facilities and a café/bar. But we really just want to see more cows in formaldehyde, please Damian. Opening times etc. hadn't been confirmed at the time we went to press, but anyone with even the slightest interest in the art world should be on tenterhooks.

Tate Modern
Bankside, SE1
(020) 7401 5000
➟ Southwark

You can't miss the looming tower of the old power station as you walk along the Thames, and since it's free to enter, (exhibitions cost extra) you won't be able to help yourself from sneaking inside. The Tate's mammoth interior is so large they had helter skelter slides between the floors last year and you could wander round the collections of international modern and contemporary art – from 1900 to the present day – for hours.

ⓒ *Sun–Thu, 10am–6pm (last admission, 5.15pm); Fri–Sat, 10am–10pm (last admission, 9.15pm)*
ⓔ *Free*

Out & about

MUSEUMS

British Museum

Great Russell Street, WC1
(020) 7323 8000
⊖ Russell Square/Holborn

Free to get in since 1753, the British Museum hides behind its doors one of the biggest collections of human cultural history in the world, from the Rosetta Stone and an Easter Island statue, to the earliest known image of Christ (nothing like the one you saw in your slice of burnt toast that time). Stand in front of the folk with sketch books. Or, try getting into as many people's photographs as possible.

🕓 *Sat–Wed, 10am–5.30pm;*
Thu–Fri, 10am–8.30pm
💲 *Free*

Design Museum

28 Shad Thames, SE1
(08709) 099 009
⊖ London Bridge/Bermondsey

Still got aspirations to become as good as Rolf Harris? You might find inspiration here. If not, you'll come away thinking you've got to rearrange your house, paint everything purple, and create seating in your living room using barbed wire and old lightbulbs. Their exhibition programme aims to capture the excitement and ingenuity of design, architecture and fashion through the 20th and 21st centuries. It's not exactly Ikea, and there are no Swedish meatballs, but there is a very nice coffee shop.

🕓 *Mon–Sun, 10am–5.45pm*
(last admission 5.15pm)
💲 *Adults, £7; concs, £4*

Football

LONDON IS HOME TO SOME OF THE FINEST TEAMS AND INDIVIDUAL PLAYERS IN THE WORLD. AND SOME FAT OLD ONES, TOO, AS EXPLAINED HERE...

Arsenal FC

Emirates Stadium, 75 Drayton Park, N5
(020) 7704 4040
⊖ **Arsenal**

One of the best-supported teams in London is Arsenal, and their spanking new Emirates Stadium is spectacular to behold. While seeing Thierry Henry and friends run rings round another Premiership team is indeed a beautiful sight, tickets are scarce, but catching a cup game is a good alternative.

Fulham FC

Craven Cottage, Stevenage Road, SW6
(08704) 421 222
⊖ **Putney Bridge**

Fulham are LDN's oldest team, and while not in the same league (ok, they are, but you catch our drift...) as the capital's big guns, their football's entertaining, and tickets are fairly cheap. Uniquely, they also have a neutral supporters' stand, but we bet even they question the ref's parentage at least twice a game.

Masters Football

www.mastersfootball.com
(020) 8952 9525

If your fondest football memories hark back to days when bad hair and tight shorts were compulsory, then check out a Masters Football game. Held regularly around London, usually at Wembley Arena, they offer a rare chance to see players like Gazza and Chris Waddle show off their silky skills while carrying a beer gut around with them.

Real football

www.football-league.premiumtv.co.uk

If you want to see some football where the players don't spend more on their haircuts than we'd pay for a small family car then check out a home game at Brentford FC, Leyton Orient, Queens Park Rangers, AFC Wimbledon or one of the other London clubs who battle their way up and down the lower leagues on a weekly basis. Check the website listed above for details.

Out & about

Natural History Museum

Cromwell Road, SW7

(020) 7942 5000

⊖ South Kensington

This is the one Itchy heads to if it wants to regress to childhood. Ross from *Friends* made dinosaurs cool again, but even before that we loved staring up at the big bones and imagining we were cavemen. Promoting the discovery, understanding, enjoyment, and responsible use of the natural world, you'll find all things big, bright and beautiful here, including world-class collections, new exhibitions and cutting-edge research to blow your bum bag off. Don't miss the ice-skating in the winter.

🕒 *Mon–Sun, 10am–5.50pm*

(last admission, 5.30pm)

🎫 *Free*

Science Museum

Exhibition Road, SW7

(08708) 704 868

⊖ South Kensington

We once got told to move on because we became so fascinated with the holograms that we were disturbing small children. But hey, with so many things to touch and play with, is it any wonder this place brings out the kid in all of us? We love the old school toy exhibition and we never tire of getting electric shocks from the giant pole in the electricity section – 'I can touch it longer than you,' we shout, elated, to our friends, as our teeth chatter and our hair stands on end. Actually it's all perfectly safe, and moreover, a fab weekend time-waster.

🕒 *Mon–Sun, 10am–6pm*

🎫 *Free*

Victoria & Albert Museum

Cromwell Road, SW7

(020) 7942 2000

⊖ South Kensington

From design and fashion to photography and architecture, the changing exhibitions here always seem to highlight the hottest stuff around. For example, the last time Itchy ventured down for an exhibition of clothing and shoes made from animal skin and feathers. Kate Moss eat your heart out (which'd be the most she's eaten in years). Seriously, this is one of the best of the bunch, and a great spot for meeting your next arty lover over a blurred photo you can both read deeper meaning into. Aaaw.

🕒 *Mon–Tue & Thu–Sun, 10am–5.45pm;*

Wed & last Fri of month, 10am–10pm

🎫 *Free*

Good sports

AS FAR AS WE'RE CONCERNED, REACHING FOR THE PACKET OF PORK SCRATCHINGS OCCASIONALLY IS MORE THAN ENOUGH EXERCISE FOR US. STILL, IF YOU HAPPEN TO BE SOME KIND OF SADIST, THEN LONDON HAS PLENTY TO OFFER. READ ON...

Wimbledon

Church Road, SW19
(020) 8971 2473
www.wimbledon.org
⊖ Southfields

The Wimbledon Championships are held 25th June–8th July, but buy tickets early or risk queuing. Once our latest tennis golden boy drops out after the first round, you may feel inspired to don the lilywhites. If so, there are numerous tennis courts around London and www.londontennis. co.uk provides an extensive directory.

Cricket

The Oval and Lords
www.surreycricket.com
www.middlesexccc.com
⊖ Oval (Oval); St John's Wood (Lords)

There's Surrey County Cricket Club residing at the Oval in South London and Lords north of the Thames, home to Middlesex County Cricket Club. And there's no sense in crying over spilt ashes, since no matter how many times the Aussies win (let's not talk about it), The Ashes will never be removed from Lords.

Running

Various venues around London, usually parks such as Regents or Hyde Park

Various running events are organised throughout the year in the big city, including several charity 10km races, the legendary London marathon and more recently, a North v South race. There is usually a blaze of publicity when the events are announced, so dash down to the Marathon Store in Covent Garden and get some new trainers before the big announcement.

Skates Cool

(07917) 400 200
Hyde Park
www.skatescool.com
⊖ Hyde Park Corner

'He was a sk8er boi, she said see you later boi.' Had he come here for private tuition, an afternoon 'crash' course, or a four week programme, his skating technique might have been a little less slapstick, and he might have earned himself a little slap 'n' tickle. Instead of just a slap in the face, before slapping into the pavement...

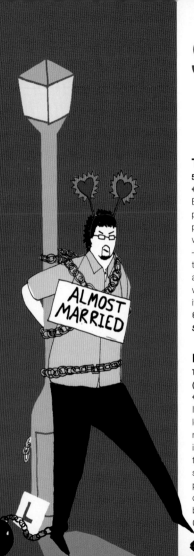

Stag &

The Langley

5 Langley Street, WC2

⊖ **Covent Garden**

Bag yourself a candlelit booth for 20 people, or a larger nook or cranny if your party's more than 50 strong. This is a rabbit warren with excitement round every corner – try the Toblerone cocktail and go straight to heaven. Bare bricks, retro décor and a decent happy hour from 5pm–7pm on weeknights with a tenner off champers – it's popular for a reason we tell ya.

🕓 *Mon–Sat, 5pm–1am;*
Sun, 4pm–10.30pm

Roadhouse

The Piazza, WC2

(020) 7836 5775

⊖ **Covent Garden**

If you've squeezed your fat arse into a pair of leggings and you've come to town for your mate's third hen night in as many years, this is the place for you. The food's pretty decent, the drinks are cheap – go for the two-for-one specials at 5.30pm – but sadly the music is pants and the crowd consists of tourists, drunks and wankers. You're probably better off in Walkabout round the corner.

🕓 *Mon–Sat, 4.30pm–3am; Sun, 4.30pm–1am*

hen nights

GET OUT THE L-PLATES, SUPER GLUE AND FAKE PLASTIC PENISES. IT'S TIME TO HELP YOUR PAL HAVE ONE LAST HOORAH/MANACLE THEM TO A LAMPPOST

Spice Lounge

124–126 Wardour Street, W1
(020) 7434 0808
⊖ Tottenham Court Road

In the middle of Soho it can be a struggle to find a place to eat past 11pm, unless you want to queue with the drunken dregs for the obvious late-night spots. Spice however, serves great Indian food (try the fish kebabs) 'til 3am and the drinks ain't half bad either – £2.50 all night, Monday to Thursday. Dance in the red and retro club 'til late, but don't lose your L-plates.

Mon–Thu, 5pm–12am; Fri-Sat, 5pm–3am

Café Corfu

7–9 Pratt Street, NW1
(020) 7424 0203
⊖ Camden Town

If the hen wants to smash a few plates and get her wedding nerves out of the way, this cute and cosy Greek spot, hidden on a side street in Camden is her dream come true. As soon as you see the belly dancer, however, you know it's going to go downhill. She'll invite you up to dance and you'll be so pissed you'll comply. Cheesy, cheeky, Greeky fun; you'll be back for more.

Times vary

Loungelover

1 Whitby Street, E2
(020) 7012 1234
⊖ Liverpool Street

If you're an arty farty type who only hangs out in bars that used to be something – ie, an old barbers, an Indian burial ground, etc – you'll love this. It used to be a meat-packing factory. They do insanely good cocktails and you'll see all sorts of gorgeous glamourpusses strutting their stuff. A great place to kick off the evening.

Tue–Thu & Sun, 6pm–12am; Fri, 6pm–1am; Sat, 7pm–1am

Tiger Tiger

29 Haymarket, SW1
(020) 7930 1885
⊖ Piccadilly

Two words: 'Chavtastic'. Or is that one word? Whatever you call it, this meat market is one to avoid at all costs, unless half your party is looking to pull on your mate's last night of freedom. The banker wankers get here early and generally stay, too pissed to move, so the late crowd consists of boozers, users and losers. And of course, tourists. London at its worst – beware.

Mon–Sat, 12pm–3am; Sun, 3pm–12am

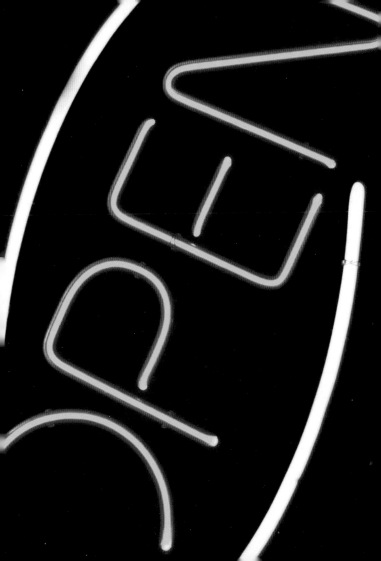

Laters

Party on. And on. And on.

London has a multitude of eclectic late-night haunts open 'til the dawning hours to keep you night owls and long distance somnambulists off the streets. Come on people, the morning-after pain's nothing that a really hot bath, a smart outfit and some moisturiser won't fix (alcoholics take note, using this technique, you can keep your boss from knowing you have a problem right up until the point where you confess your alcoholism in a best-selling city guide that he publishes). Prepare yourself for a caffeine fix in the morning because these places are seriously worth losing shuteye over. Take it from us. Our bodies didn't sleep deprive themselves, you know.

Named after the Hungarian composer, Bartok (78–79 Chalk Farm Road, NW1, 020 7916 0595, Chalk Farm tube) is a seductive, sexy space to chill and indulge in some late night culture. The music is a mixture of classical, ambient electronica and lazy chill-out grooves, which totally fits the romantic, rouge interior. The place is open until 3am from Sun–Thu and 4am on a weekend, which pretty much makes it the perfect venue for an extended date.

If, however, you fancy something a tad more upbeat, head to the kitsch cavern that is Janet's Bar (30 Old Brompton Road, SW7, 020 7581 3160, South Kensington tube). This New Yorker will make you feel at home quicker than you can say 'photomontage' – which, incidentally, is what makes up the wallpaper of the entire bar. Make sure you leave your airs and graces at the door (but don't forget you wallet – the prices are the only clue to its locality), order a Harvey Wallbanger and settle in 'til 1am (2am Fri–Sat). If you're into late night gabbing and making brand new friends, then this is the place for you.

For those in search of some serious cool factor, Beduin is the only option (57–59 Charterhouse Street, Smithfield, EC1, 020 7336 6484, Farringdon tube). Open from 12pm–4am during week and 5am on weekends, the three-level maroon interior is adorned with more Moroccan artefacts than you'd find in a camel-drover's living room, but attracts exactly the kind of sophisticated clientele that a hashish dealer's never going to get. Adorned with sofas and floor cushions, the basement features an in-house DJ playing funky house tunes – perfect for chic nocturnal gatherings with a group of your stylish mates.

Laters

If you're feeling the North African vibe but in the mood for something a bit more chilled, then Café Cairo is your place (88 Landor Road, Clapham, SW9, 020 7771 1201, Clapham North tube). Amazingly unknown amongst Claphamites, this Arabic den bubbles with aromas of flavoured tobacco and Turkish coffee, and oozes an exotic, laid-back atmosphere. Well, we say it's 'amazingly' unknown; actually we suspect touches like the weirdly cramped men's latrines (they can only be described as latrines), and dingy, smoky atmosphere, combined with the posho sensibilities of most of the residents of the area might have something to do with it. Also, anyone taller than Ronnie Corbett may suffer minor discomfort as bed-style seating in the corner tends to go very quickly, meaning your bum-parking options generally consist of low-level chairs and ankle-high tables. Still, hook yourself up to a shisha pipe and let your cares drift away until the very early hours, and you're unlikely to care. Especiallly as it'll mean that you can spend a few hours free from all the rugby-shirted estate agents. NB, rugby-shirted estate agents may want to head to Mosquito Bar (5 Clapham High Street, SW4, Clapham North tube). You'll love it in there.

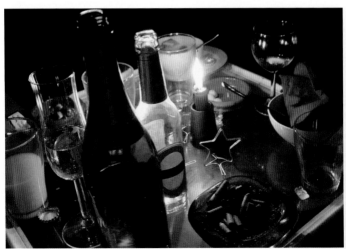

Fun @ night

DON'T WASTE THE GIFT OF INSOMNIA BY COUNTING IMAGINARY ANIMALS – GO CREATE SOME SHEAR (ARF) MAYHEM IN THE EARLY AM AND ENTER THE ITCHY TWILIGHT ZONE. WE WOOL IF YOU WOOL

Go jousting – First up, feed up for some insane-sbury's prices. As witching hours approach, 24-hour supermarkets reduce any unsold fresh produce to mere coppers; pick up a feast for a few pauper's pennies and buy them clean out of 10p French sticks, which are spot on for sword fights. Up the ante by jousting using shopping trolleys or bicycles in place of horses, or start a game of ciabatta-and-ball by bowling a roll.

Play street games – Take some chalk to sketch a marathon hopscotch grid down the entire length of the thoroughfare, or an anaconda-sized snakes and ladders board writhing across your town square. Break the trippy silence and deserted stillness of the dead shopping areas with a tag, catch or British bulldog competition, and be as rowdy as you like – there's no-one around to wake.

Play Texaco bingo – Alternatively, drive the cashier at the all-night petrol station honey nut loopy by playing Texaco bingo: the person who manages to make them go back and forth from the window the most times to fetch increasingly obscure, specific and embarrassing items wins. Along with your prize-winning haul of mango chutney-flavoured condoms, Tena Lady towelettes and tin of eucalyptus travel sweets, be sure to pick up a first-edition paper to trump everyone over toast with your apparently psychic knowledge of the day ahead's events-to-be. Whatever you do, remember: you snooze, you lose.

Illustration by Thomas Denbigh

Body

Body & living

SPA

Agua at the Sanderson
50 Berners Street, W1
(020) 7300 1400
⊖ Oxford Circus

Apparently it's Britney's fave when she's in town, which, let's face it, probably isn't terribly often these days, unless she's fleeing a child custody case, or being badly advised by new bezzie mate Paris to go on another 'profile boosting' bender. Nonetheless, it's a great place to spot the celebs who can still afford the shocking £80 price tag for a 55 minute massage. It looks like you *can* put a price on pure pleasure, after all. Just ask Ms Spears – four quid for a supersize Big Mac meal.
🕒 *Spa, Mon–Sun, 7am–9pm; gym, open 24 hours for members and hotel guests*

Mayfair Spa
Stratton Street, W1
(020) 7915 2626
⊖ Green Park

Despite the fact that we've often felt the game to be oddly unfair to Angel Islington, there's a reason that Mayfair's the most expensive square on the Monopoly board, you know. With seven treatment rooms, a mud spa for your inner hippo, a steam chamber, plus a herbal steam room, this little boudoir is quieter than most central spas and offers group bookings for the perfect weekend with your mates. Great for a hen day – look for special offers. Head straight there, and do not pass 'Go', although as it isn't the cheapest, you may still wish to collect £200.
🕒 *Times vary*

Ironmonger Row Baths
1–11 Ironmonger Row, EC1
(020) 7253 4011
⊖ Old Street

This beautiful art deco building houses a 30.5 metre modern swimming pool, steam rooms, hot rooms, and for the really daring among you, there's also an icy plunge pool. Come for an exercise and a rub-down, or alternatively, you can just snooze on a bed and marvel at the relaxed atmosphere, enjoyed by mums with babies, students and senior citizens alike. A bargain eight quid will get you four hours in the baths, although a body scrub or massage (which can be booked in advance) will cost you extra.
🕒 *Mon–Fri, 6.30am–9pm; Sat, 9am–6pm; Sun, 10am–6pm*

The Porchester Spa Turkish Baths

Porchester Centre, Queensway, W2

(020) 7792 3980

⊖ Royal Oak

It might be old but they did such a good refurb that unless your detective skills are so good that you spend a lot of your spare time in a dirty mac chomping on cigars, muttering 'just one more thing,' you'll never be able to tell. What's more, it's probably the best place to get your steam on if you're on a budget. Look out for the late night parties when men, women, and even OAPs come chasing a good time. No wait, it's not like that... what kind of guide do you think this is? We'd never recommend an orgy which allows entrance to OAPs. Well, not unless they were *really* sexy.

Mon–Sun, 10am–10pm

The Sanctuary

12 Floral Street, WC2

(08707) 703 350

⊖ Covent Garden

A feminine world of peace and tranquillity? No, sisters, sadly it's not an ice cream-filled swimming pool, soundtracked by *Careless Whisper* and patrolled by Brad Pitt lookalikes in Speedos. It is in fact a spa just a skip away from the busy Covent Garden piazza. Who'd have thought it? As a spa with one of the best reps in the capital, as well as a range of facial treatments, body wraps, flotation tanks and exfoliation, you'll wonder exactly how it was that you ever managed to get by without it. Although you're probably wondering about that ice cream pool more, now.

Mon–Tue, 9.30am–6pm; Wed–Fri. 9.30am–10pm; Sat–Sun, 9.30am–8pm

The Walk in Back Rub

14 Neal's Yard, WC2

(020) 7836 9111

⊖ Covent Garden

Unlike most massages we've had, where we've been asked to strip off and lie down, (er, they were massage parlours, weren't they?) the treatment at this Neal's Yard trinket involves you sitting in a chair for ten minutes, fully clothed, and letting an expert rub away your woes. A far better way to spend your lunch break than ramming your person through the Covent Garden crowds if you work here. And if you're shopping? Well, ditch that heavy load for a moment... aaah.

Mon–Sat, 11.30am–7pm; Sun, 1am–6pm

€ £9.75 for 10 minutes

Body & living

HAIRDRESSERS

Burlingtons

Cavendish Square, 14 John Princes Street, W1

(08708) 701 299

⊖ Oxford Circus

Considering they offer a cut, mini manicure, facial, makeover and photo shoot all for the price of your average high street number, you have to ask yourself why you wouldn't head here. The answer is either that you want skin that fits your face like a deflated beachball around a tangerine, or you're a fool. It may take a while, but the constant Bucks Fizz helps, although it won't do you any favours when it comes to the photo shoot.

🕐 *Mon–Fri, 8.45am–8pm; Sat, 9am–8pm; Sun, 10am–6pm*

💷 *Experience package, £39*

The Refinery

60 Brook Street, W1

(020) 7409 2001

⊖ Bond Street

An all-male grooming salon, The Refinery offers old-fashioned smooth shaves, massages, hair removal and skincare sessions alongside other things for the metrosexual gentleman. The dark wood décor, calm atmosphere and beautiful fstaff make the place seem slightly more macho than the brochure would suggest, but we guess that given the effeminate nature of the venue, some fellas might feel they need it. They do gift vouchers and also sell the lotions and potions they use. A place to get swanky treats for yourself or the man in your life.

🕐 *Mon–Tue, 10am–7pm; Wed–Fri, 10am–9pm; Sat, 9am–6pm; Sun, 11am–5pm*

Ginger Group House of Hair and Beauty

43 High Street, W5

(020) 8567 5264/8760

⊖ Ealing Broadway

They say that where there's no pain there's no gain, but with the beautiful Mitch determined to reach every nook and cranny, you'll be the best-kept lady (or man) in town. This spot is head to toe beauty, from the usual haircut and colour, manicure and massage, right through to photo facials and laser hair removal. Leave your nose plucking to the experts, folks.

🕐 *Mon–Fri, 9am–7.30pm; Sat, 9am–6pm; Sun, 10am–5pm*

💷 *Full leg & bikini wax from £22, basic cut & colour £80, laser hair removal on quotation (bikini line from £50 per session)*

Rush

25 Strutton Ground, SW1

(08002) 983 212

⊖ Victoria

You know how oldies like to bang on about how the youth of today are always in a rush? Well, this is the joint they're talking about. A relatively new kid on the block, these trendy salons have cool written all over them (not literally – that'd just be blowing their own trumpet). The staff are always gorgeous too, and they're surprisingly willing to squeeze you in on a lunch break, or at least give you a free fringe trim if the indie locks have turned a tad unruly. We like. Other locations are Covent Garden, Putney and Wimbledon.

🕐 *Mon–Fri, 9am–8pm; Sat, 9am–6.30pm*

💷 *Women's cut, £30–£50*

Body & living

GYMS

Fitness First
Various locations
(08708) 988 080

Yeah, yeah, so you all know the drill with these places. They're not the swankiest, and if you're a member you'll devote significant amounts of time to whingeing about having your nose up Vicky Pollard's armpit as you fight for the free weights, but at least it gets the job done. Plus, what with Itchy's Uncle Tony having schooled us throughout our youth about how sitting over the road from one of these was the best way to check out totty, there's at least some painless benefits to the place. So long as you don't end up wincing at the mingers.

🕙 *Times vary according to branch*

Soho Gym
193 Camden High Street, NW1
(020) 7482 4524
⊖ **Camden Town**

You might be wondering exactly what somewhere called Soho Gym is doing located in Camden, but surprise, surprise, it's a chain with locations all over town. It's a firm fave with London's fashionistas and all those eagerly awaiting the arrival of a record producer right next to them on the adjacent treadmill. What's more, with there being no joining fee or contracts to sign, you can come and go as quickly as the clientele's fashionable eating disorders.

💷 *Membership including all gym activities, sauna and studio classes start from £30 a month; day and week visitor passes also available*

The Third Space
13 Sherwood Street, W1
(020) 7439 7333
⊖ **Piccadilly Circus**

Book your spinning class online as you leave work, then after you've done more spinning around than even Kylie could handle, swim a few lengths of backstroke as you gaze through the glass ceiling at the amazing Thai Boxing going on above. There's loads of equipment and classes, from a climbing wall, via a medical centre offering massage and acupuncture, right through to counselling, laundry service, and free wifi. Who needs a flat? We can all move in here.

🕙 *Mon–Fri, 6.30am–11pm;*
Sat & Sun, 8.30am–8.30pm
💷 *£118 a month*

ALTERNATIVE

Shymala Ayurveda
152 Holland Park Avenue, W11
(020) 7348 0018
⊖ Holland Park

Voted as one of the top health centres in the country by a magazine that knows its stuff, this Hyde Park hot spot offers hippy-ish... erm, we mean *holistic* health and spa treatments like Pristhabhyanga (try saying *that* three times quickly), which apparently is an exhilarating back massage using herbs. Personally, we'd probably feel just as good if we took a bath with a pot of dried parsley (unless someone mistook us for a stew, of course) but these people seem to know what they're doing.

🕑 *Mon–Fri, 9am–7pm; Sat, 9am–5pm*

Bar Salsa!
96 Charing Cross Road, WC2
(020) 7379 3277
⊖ Leicester Square

Despite the fact this place is located slap bang in the middle of tourist world, fortunately this slice of Spain is surprisingly free of massive gangs of shiny-shoed, shouty pissheads. Head down on Fridays for a free introduction to Latin dancing from 6.30pm, and you can tuck into some of their tasty grub, too. That's right, not only can you tippity-tap around the bar, but afterwards you can gorge yourself on tippity-top tasty tapas. What's that? You reckon that last sentence is a bit of mouthful? You should try the food here then...

🕑 *7pm–8pm, £2; 8pm–9pm, £4; 9pm–11pm, £8; after 11pm, £10*

OTHER

The Art of Erotic Dance

The Basement Dance Studio,
400 York Way, York House, N7
(020) 7700 7722
⊖ Caledonian Road

Like that Barbie doll you abused as a kid, it's your turn to be erotically bent and moved in all the right places (erm, not that we did that, you understand – we've just heard that some oddball kids used to do that kind of thing). Intended to help women build up self-confidence, this class guarantees that they'll enhance your sensuality, teach you erotic dance routines and help you have fun with feathers, hats and props, (as if you needed it – these people obviously never had a Barbie).

🕒 *Call for opening hours and class times*

London Fencing Club

Various Venues
www.londonfencingclub.co.uk

Foxes making a mess of your bin bags? Tramps keep making homes for themselves in your rockery? Then you need to get these guys to come take a look at your fences. Sorry? Ohhh, we're talking *that* kind of fencing. Silly us. Well, if meshing yourself up to the nines and running around with a big sharp stick is your thing, then you'll be pleased to know there are other weirdos gathering regularly to get their kicks out of this ancient fighting form. With classes for all abilities, from total beginners through to expert swordsmen, you can learn enough skills to teach those foxes/tramps a pointy lesson, whatever your level.

🎫 *Membership from £35 per month*

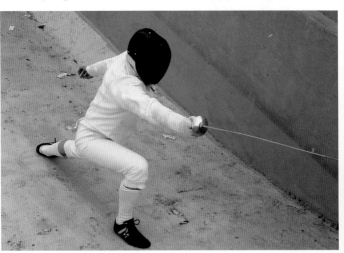

IF YOU'RE AFTER GUILTY PLEASURES, WHY NOT GO FOR THE CLASSICS? NO, NOT PROSTITUTION AND PICKING YOUR SCABS, BUT HOTDOGS AND ILLEGAL MINICABS

There are guilty pleasures to be had in London at any time of day, but it's at night that it really comes into its own. Don't believe us? Then try Cheapskates (Wed, Moonlighting, 17 Greek Street, W1, 020 7437 5782). Cheesier than David Hasselhoff's sock drawer, getting so smashed on 60p shots that you can't see, and rocking out to *Come On Eileen* just ain't cool, but damn it, it's fun.

And the questionably shameful temptations don't end there. Come home-time, an army of connective tissue pimps are waiting for you, lurking on street corners, frying onions to tempt you into eating one of their sweaty, gristle-stuffed tubes of pestilence. You'd normally steer clear of eating something with the nutritional value of a dog's scrotum, but when you're drunk enough to have played tonsil hockey with a Mandy Dingle lookalike, anything goes. What's more, they'll leave you with enough change to get a minicab home in time to vom it all up again.

Guilty
pleasures

Illustration by Si Clark
www.si-clark.co.uk

Sleep

Sleep

SWANKY

The Landmark London
222 Marylebone Road, NW1
(020) 7631 8000
⊖ Marylebone
This place reels in celebs and people with lots of money like trout to sweetcorn.
🛏 *Double room, from £241 per night*

Plaza on the River
18 Albert Embankment, SE1
(020) 7769 2525
⊖ Vauxhall
Facing the Tate, this is one of London's most impressive hotels. Take a dip in your enormous tub, drink the mini-bar dry and snuggle up in your pimping bath robe.
🛏 *Double room, from £141 per night*

The Ritz
150 Piccadilly, W1
(020) 7493 8181
⊖ Piccadilly Circus
Still standing after a century and still serving London's priciest tea, you'll need a second mortgage to stay here. With two staff members per guest, you'll be spoilt rotten.
🛏 *Double room, from £294 per night*

The Rookery
Cowcross Street, EC1
(020) 7336 0931
⊖ Farringdon
It's the mansion you'll never own but will wander through eternally in your dreams. Gorgeous furnishings, glitzy staff who love to help, and fine dining to boot. Bring it on.
🛏 *Double room, from £119 per night*

The Sanderson
50 Berners Street, W1
(020) 7300 1400
⊖ Tottenham Court Road
It's Britney's fave place to play pool in London, apparently. The rooms are whiter than Simon Cowell's teeth and the lift's more spacey than Kevin.
🛏 *Double room, from £282 per night*

The Savoy
The Strand, WC2
(020) 7836 4343
⊖ Charing Cross
You know in the movies, where they have things like rooftop pools and a man playing the piano as two lovers dine together? Well that all happens here. We think.
🛏 *Double room, from £199 per night*

MID-RANGE

Carlton Hotel
90 Belgrave Road, SW1
(020) 7976 6634
⊖ Pimlico

This place is near Victoria, which makes it perfect for train and bus-spotters.

🛏 *Double room, from £93 per night*

Devonport House
King William Walk, Greenwich, SE10
(020) 8269 5400
⊖ Cutty Sark (DLR)

Often used for corporate dos, there's more atmosphere under an old copy of *London Lite* left on a bus. The Admiral's Lounge is good for a monstrous G & T though.

🛏 *Double room, from £89 per night*

Hyde Park Towers
41–51 Inverness Terrace, Bayswater, W2
(020) 7221 8484
⊖ Bayswater

Imagine you're a posh Victorian in a huge frock as you wander back to bed through tree-lined streets after an evening's dancing. Frilly umbrella optional.

🛏 *Double room, from £89 per night*

Mentone Hotel
54–56 Cartwright Gardens, WC1
(020) 7387 3927
⊖ Russell Square

With its pretty, pastel-painted rooms, the Mentone will charm your pants off if you can bag a room overlooking the gardens and the tennis courts. London? Where's that?

🛏 *Double room, from £95 per night*

NH Harrington Hall
5–25 Harrington Gardens, SW7
(020) 7396 9696
⊖ Gloucester Road

Right down to the floral curtains, you couldn't get more English if you tried. Mingle with the fashionistas in the posh bits of Chelsea, and don't forget to visit the sauna.

🛏 *Double room, from £85 per night*

Novotel London
10 Pepys Street, EC3
(020) 7265 6000
⊖ Tower Hill

This basic chain hotel will do you for a few nights if you can handle the city boys pouring out of Wetherspoons and into the pants of their co-workers late at night. Loudly.

🛏 *Double room, from £99 per night*

CHEAP

EasyHotel

14 Lexham Gardens, W8

www.easyhotel.com

⊖ Gloucester Road

Cheapo rooms for those with a love of the colour orange. And greek entrepreneurs.

💶 *Double room, from £25 per night*

The Fitzroy B&B Hotel

41 Fitzroy Street, W1

(020) 7387 7919

⊖ Great Portland Street

Comfy B&B with en-suite rooms. Close to the West End with a lovely atmosphere – it's like having tea with your family, only you're not quite sure who let the backpacker in.

💶 *Double room, from £60 per night*

Holland Park YHA

Holland Park, W8

(020) 7937 0748

⊖ Holland Park

The best of bargain beds in town, with a view worthy of royalty (literally). A great place to meet someone to wander into town with. We're considering living here full-time.

💶 *Beds, from £27 per night*

St Pancras YHA

78–81 Euston Road, NW1

(020) 7388 9998

⊖ King's Cross St Pancras

You don't have to go bankrupt for a decent night's kip, and here's the proof. It's cheap, but comfortable, and about 15 minutes walk from any place in central London.

💶 *Beds, from £27 per night*

Grenville Hotel

4 Guilford Street, WC1

(020) 7405 9470

⊖ Russell Square

You know it's old school if it comes with a trouser press, and here there's one in every room (gasp). Itchy loves the bright yellow walls, especially in winter.

💶 *Double room, from £69 per night*

Holland Court Hotel

Holland Court, W14

(020) 7371 1133

⊖ Kensington (Olympia)

Itchy's a massive fan of anything boutique style, and this hotel close to Earl's Court and Olympia is not only fab, but the price also includes a massive breakfast. Bonus.

💶 *Double room, from £55 per night*

Tudor Court Hotel

10–12 Norfolk Square, W2

(020) 7723 6553

⊖ Paddington

This hotel was built in the 1850s, long before kebab shops were invented. Close to Hyde Park, shut out the modern London and talk to the trees instead.

💶 *Double room, from £65 per night*

University of London Halls

Various locations in central London

(020) 7862 8880

It's best not to know about some things. Like not knowing what's taken place on your mattress, what died in your shower, and what caused the suspicious stain on the carpet. Still, you get what you pay for, eh?

💶 *Rooms, from £20 per night*

Baltis in Birmingham?
Cocktails in Cardiff?
Gigs in Glasgow?

If you're starting from scratch,
you'd better get Itchy.

For the best features and reviews of where
to go out all over the UK, log on to:

www.itchycity.co.uk

Bath/Birmingham/Brighton/Bristol/Cambridge/Cardiff/Edinburgh/
Glasgow/Leeds/Liverpool/London/Manchester/
Nottingham/Oxford/Sheffield/York

Useful info

Useful info

INTERNET CAFÉS

Battersea Net
40 St John's Hill, SW11
(020) 7738 0015
⊖ Clapham Junction (BR)

easyInternetcafé
358 Oxford Street, W1
⊖ Bond Street

easyInternetcafé
112–114 Camden High Street, NW1
⊖ Camden Town/Mornington Crescent

Café Internet
22–24 Buckingham Palace Road, SW1
(020) 7233 5786
⊖ Victoria

Momo Internet Café
208 Brick Lane, E1
(020) 7739 5196
⊖ Shoreditch/Liverpool Street

Netstream
9–12 St Anne's Court, W1
(020) 7434 2525
⊖ Tottenham Court Road/Leicester Square

Rex Lounge
30 Woburn Place, WC1
(020) 7637 4545
⊖ Russell Square/Euston

Urban Connexions
24 Fortess Road, NW5
(020) 7267 2922
⊖ Kentish Town

TRAINS

Southern Railway
(08451) 272 920

Eurostar
(08705) 186 186

First Great Western
(08457) 000 125

GNER
(08457) 225 225

National Rail Enquiries
(08457) 484 950

Virgin Trains
(08457) 222 333

TAXIS

Addison Lee
(020) 7387 8888

Cabwise
Text 'HOME' to 60835

Radio Cars
(020) 7916 2121

Premier Cars
(020) 7226 8988

CAR HIRE

Budget
(0800) 581 2233
www.budget.co.uk

TRAVEL

Catamaran Cruisers
(020) 7987 1185

London Transport Info Line
(020) 7222 1234

London Transport Lost Property Office
200 Baker Street, NW1
(08453) 309 882
⊖ Baker Street
🕐 *Mon–Fri 8.30am–4pm*

Victoria Coach Station
164 Buckingham Palace Road, SW1
(020) 7730 3466
⊖ Victoria

PLANES

Gatwick
(08700) 002 468
⊖ Victoria (Gatwick Express)

Heathrow
(08700) 000 123
⊖ Heathrow Terminals 1, 2, 3/Heathrow Terminal 4/
Paddington (Heathrow Express)

London City
(020) 7646 0088
⊖ London City Airport (DLR)

Stansted
(08700) 000 303
⊖ Liverpool Street/Tottenham Hale (BR)
(Stansted Express)

FOOD DELIVERY

Deliverance
(08000) 191 111
Freshly cooked food delivery service.

www.roomservice.co.uk
(020) 7644 6666
Deliver from top restaurants to your door.

ORIENTAL DELIVERY

Feng Sushi Fulham
218 Fulham Road, SW10
(020) 7795 1900

Feng Sushi Southwark
13 Stoney Street, SE1
(020) 7407 8744

PIZZA DELIVERY

Basilico
175 Lavender Hill, SW15
(08003) 899 770
www.basilico.co.uk
Wood-fired pizzas with fresh toppings, made in mere minutes for your salivating chops. Pizza the way God intended.

Domino's Pizza
89 Charlwood Street, SW1
(020) 7834 2211
www.dominos.co.uk
Might be a chain, but they come up trumps time and time again. The Dominator will leave you feeling dirrrty in a way Christina Aguilera can only dream about. Check out the website to order online.

The Broadway Pizza
9 Camden High Street, NW1
(020) 7383 5010

Papa John's Pizza
178 Upper Street, N1
(020) 7354 3003

Pizza Hut
454 Edgware Road, W2
(020) 7723 8883

Royal Pizza
1 King's Cross Bridge, N1
(020) 7837 5777

Snappy Tomato Pizza
174 Earl's Court Road, SW5
(020) 7373 4433

Support

Illustration by Joly Braime

Citizens' Advice Bureaux
(020) 8892 5917
www.citizensadvice.org.uk

24hr London Dentist Helpline
(07074) 455 999

Charing Cross Hospital A&E
Fulham Palace Road, W6
(020) 8846 1234

Family Planning Association
(020) 7608 5240
🕒 Mon–Fri, 9am–7pm

LGB Counselling
(020) 7837 3337

Pharmacy (24 hr)
233–235 Old Brompton Road, SW5
(020) 7373 2798

Police
(020) 7713 1212
www.met.police.uk/tourist

Rape
Victim Support London
(020) 7928 0498
🕒 Mon–Fri, 9am–5pm

Safety Advice
www.visitlondon.co.uk/city_guide/
essential_information/staying_safe

Licensed Minicab Hotline
(08718) 718 710

Itchy tube tips

Talk to Paul Weller about going underground, and he'll tell you that 'the public wants what the public gets'. Which presumably means that if we gave you a handy selection of places to go to near every Zone 1 and 2 tube station as well as a few Zone 3-ers, you'd be lapping it up. Lucky we have done then. Read on for all the gubbins you could possibly need on where to find your hangover breakfast, power lunch, hearty dinner or a late drink, whichever tube stop you happen to stumble out of. Travelcards at the ready, and don't blame us if you end up missing the last tube home, and find yourself having to sleep on a platform.

🔵 ALDGATE	🔵 ALDGATE EAST	🔵 ANGEL	🔵 ARCHWAY
BREKKIE Judy's	**BREKKIE Beigel Bake**	**BREKKIE Alpino**	**BREKKIE Toll Gate**
86 Whitechapel High St	159 Brick Ln	97 Chapel Mkt	6 Archway Cl
(020) 7375 1636	(020) 7729 0616	(020) 7837 8330	(020) 7687 2066
LUNCH Barcelona Tapas	**LUNCH Little Bay**	**LUNCH Elk in the Woods**	**LUNCH Nid Ting**
15 St Botolph St	76 Commercial St	39 Camden Psg	533 Holloway Rd
(020) 7377 5111	(020) 7247 1081	(020) 7226 3535	(020) 7263 0506
DINNER The Dickens Inn	**DINNER Sweet & Spicy**	**DINNER Giraffe**	**DINNER The Rose & Crown**
St Katharine's Dock	40 Brick Ln	29–31 Essex Rd	86 Highgate High St
(020) 7488 2208	(020) 7247 1081	(020) 7359 5999	(020) 8340 6712
DRINK The Golden Heart	**DRINK Vibe Bar**	**DRINK The Angelic**	**DRINK The Flask**
110 Commercial St	91–95 Brick Ln	57 Liverpool Rd	77 Highgate West Hl
(020) 7257 2158	(020) 7377 2899	(020) 7278 8433	(020) 8348 7346

🔵 ARSENAL	🔵 BAKER STREET	🔵 BANK	🔵 BARBICAN
BREKKIE Judy's	**BREKKIE Café Arizona**	**BREKKIE Café**	**BREKKIE Smiths**
249 Holloway Rd	134 Marylebone St	20 Little Britain	67–77 Charterhouse St
No phone	(020) 7935 0858	(020) 7355 4489	(020) 7251 7950
LUNCH Golden Fish Bar	**LUNCH Fabrizio**	**LUNCH Browns**	**LUNCH Cicada**
98 Gillespie Rd	10 Paddington St	8 Old Jewry	171 Farringdon Rd
(020) 7359 8364	(020) 7224 2556	(020) 7606 6677	(020) 7608 1550
DINNER Iznik	**DINNER Galvin**	**DINNER 1 Lombard St**	**DINNER Moro**
19 Highbury Pk	66 Baker St	1 Lombard St	34–36 Exmouth Mkt
(020) 7354 5697	(020) 7935 4007	(020) 7929 6611	(020) 7833 8336
DRINK Highbury Barn	**DRINK The Globe**	**DRINK City Tup**	**DRINK Barley Mow**
26 Highbury Pk	43–47 Marylebone Rd	66 Gresham St	50 Long Ln
(020) 7226 2383	(020) 7935 6368	(020) 7606 8176	(020) 7606 6591

🔵 BARONS COURT	🔵 BAYSWATER	🔵 BELSIZE PARK	🔵 BERMONDSEY
BREKKIE C'est Ici	**BREKKIE Café Fresco**	**BREKKIE Chamomile**	**BREKKIE Food Junkie**
47 Palliser Rd	25 Westbourne Grv	45 England's Ln	168 Jamaica Rd
(020) 7381 4837	(020) 7221 2355	(020) 7586 4580	(020) 7237 9416
LUNCH Harvest Brasserie	**LUNCH Khan's**	**LUNCH Giacobazzi's Deli**	**LUNCH The Garrison**
149 North End Rd	13–15 Westbourne Grv	150 Fleet Rd	99–101 Bermondsey St
(020) 7602 2591	(020) 7727 5420	(020) 7267 7222	(020) 7089 9355
DINNER Cibo	**DINNER Tiroler Hut**	**DINNER Weng Wah House**	**DINNER Arancia**
3 Russell Gdns	27 Westbourne Grv	240 Haverstock Hl	52 Southwark Pk Rd
(020) 7371 2085	(020) 7727 3981	(020) 7431 8620	(020) 7237 3608
DRINK Queen's Head	**DRINK Rat & Parrot**	**DRINK The White Horse**	**DRINK The Angel**
13 Brook Grn	99 Queensway	154 Fleet Rd	101 Bermondsey Wall
(020) 7603 3174	(020) 7727 0259	(020) 7485 2112	(020) 7237 3608

□□□□□□□□□□□□□□□■□

⬦ BETHNAL GREEN

BREKKIE E Pellici's
332 Bethnal Green Rd
(020) 7739 4873
LUNCH Wild Cherry
241–245 Globe Rd
(020) 8980 6678
DINNER The Fish Plaice
86 Cambridge Heath Rd
(020) 7790 3254
DRINK Pleasure Unit
359 Bethnal Green Rd
(020) 7729 0167

⬦ BLACKFRIARS

BREKKIE Bon Appetit IV
181 Queen Victoria St
(020) 7236 0305
LUNCH Stamfords
7–8 Milroy Wlk
(020) 7633 0256
DINNER Oxo Tower
Barge House St
(020) 7803 3888
DRINK The Blackfriar
174 Queen Victoria St
(020) 7236 5474

⬦ BOND STREET

BREKKIE Snack Bar
22 Brooks Mws
(020) 7629 0425
LUNCH Carluccio's
St Christopher's Pl
(020) 7935 5927
DINNER La Tasca
30–34 James St
(020) 7486 3314
DRINK Lamb & Flag
24 James St
(020) 7408 0132

⬦ BOROUGH

BREKKIE Riva
Borough High St
(020) 7407 0737
LUNCH Fish!
Cathedral St
(020) 7407 3803
DINNER Tower Tandoori
74–76 Tower Bridge Rd
(020) 7237 3126
DRINK The George Inn
77 Borough High St
(020) 7407 2056

⬦ BOW ROAD

BREKKIE Hi Way Cafe
181 Bow Rd
(020) 8983 4959
LUNCH The Crown
223 Grove Rd
(020) 8981 9998
DINNER Venus in the Park
552 Mile End Rd
(020) 8880 6634
DRINK Lord Tredegar
50 Lichfield Rd
(020) 8983 0130

⬦ BRIXTON

BREKKIE SW9
11 Dorrell Pl
(020) 7738 3116
LUNCH Lounge
88 Atlantic Rd
(020) 7733 5229
DINNER Asmara
386 Coldharbour Ln
(020) 7737 4144
DRINK Living
443 Coldharbour Ln
(020) 7326 4040

⬦ CALEDONIAN RD

BREKKIE Parma Cafe
153 York Way
(020) 7485 7609
LUNCH Milan
52 Caledonian Rd
(020) 7278 3812
DINNER My Kitchen
239 Caledonian Rd
(020) 7278 3888
DRINK Shillibeer's
Carpenters Mws
(020) 7700 1858

⬦ CAMDEN TOWN

BREKKIE Bar Gansa
2 Inverness St
(020) 7267 8909
LUNCH Stables Market
Chalk Farm Rd
No phone
DINNER Jamon Jamon
38 Parkway
(020) 7284 0606
DRINK The Dublin Castle
94 Parkway
(020) 7485 1773

⬦ CANADA WATER

BREKKIE Food Junkie
168 Jamaica Rd
(020) 7237 9416
LUNCH GB Kebabs
153 Lower Rd
(020) 7237 8064
DINNER Il Bordello
81 Wapping St
(020) 7481 9950
DRINK Spice Island
163 Rotherhithe St
(020) 7394 7108

⬦ CANARY WHARF

BREKKIE Fresco Cafe
15 Cabot Sq
(020) 7512 9072
LUNCH Singapore Sam
Cabot Place West
(020) 7513 2754
DINNER Carluccio's
2 Nash Ct
(020) 7719 1749
DRINK The Grape
76 Narrow St
(020) 7987 4396

⬦ CANNON STREET

BREKKIE Insalata
122 Cannon St
(020) 7283 7776
LUNCH Sweetings
39 Queen Victoria St
(020) 7248 3062
DINNER Fifteen 05
All Hallows Ln
(020) 7283 1505
DRINK The Cannon
95 Cannon St
(020) 7397 9881

⬦ CHALK FARM

BREKKIE Trojka
101 Regent's Pk Rd
(020) 7483 3765
LUNCH Marine Ices
8 Haverstock Hl
(020) 7482 9003
DINNER Cottons Rhum
55 Chalk Farm Rd
(020) 7482 1096
DRINK The Enterprise
2 Haverstock Hl
(020) 7485 2659

⬦ CHANCERY LANE

BREKKIE Tiffin's
24 Leather Ln
(020) 7404 5894
LUNCH Traditional Plaice
83 Leather Ln
(020) 7405 8277
DINNER Aki Japanese
182 Gray's Inn Rd
(020) 7837 9281
DRINK Ye Olde Mitre
1 Ely Ct
(020) 7405 4751

⬦ CHARING CROSS

BREKKIE Ha! Ha! Bar
6 Villiers St
(020) 7930 1263
LUNCH Thai Square
148 The Strand
(020) 7497 0904
DINNER Paradiso & Inferno
389 The Strand
(020) 7836 7491
DRINK Gordon's
47 Villiers St
(020) 7930 1408

⬦ CLAPHAM COMM

BREKKIE Gastro
67 Venn St
(020) 7627 0222
LUNCH Pepper Tree
19 Clapham Common
(020) 7622 1758
DINNER Kasbah
73 Venn St
(020) 7498 3622
DRINK SO:UK
165 Clapham High St
(020) 7622 4004

⬦ CLAPHAM NORTH

BREKKIE Mario's Café
122 Clapham High St
No phone
LUNCH Alba
3 Bedford Rd
(020) 7733 3636
DINNER La Gruta Café
91 Landor Rd
(020) 7738 7392
DRINK Bread and Roses
68 Clapham Manor St
(020) 7498 1779

Tube tips

CLAPHAM SOUTH
BREKKIE **Fuel**
27 Balham Hill
(020) 8675 5333
LUNCH **Pizza on the Green**
4 Cavendish Pde
(020) 8673 3227
DINNER **Bombay Bicycle**
95 Nightingale Ln
(020) 8673 6217
DRINK **The Abbeville**
67 Abbeville Rd
(020) 8675 2201

COVENT GARDEN
BREKKIE **Frank's Café**
52 Neal St
(020) 7863 6345
LUNCH **Fire & Stone**
31 32 Maiden Ln
(020) 7257 8613
DINNER **Africa Centre**
38 King St
(020) 7836 1976
DRINK **The Lamb & Flag**
33 Rose St
(020) 7497 9504

EARL'S COURT
BREKKIE **Troubadour**
265 Old Brompton Rd
(020) 7370 1434
LUNCH **Krungtap**
227 Old Brompton Rd
(020) 7259 2314
DINNER **The Little French**
18 Hogarth Pl
(020) 7370 0366
DRINK **Balans West**
249 Old Brompton Rd
(020) 7244 8838

EAST PUTNEY
BREKKIE **A Quick One**
3 Keswick Bdwy
(020) 8874 5785
LUNCH **La Mancha**
32 Putney High St
(020) 8780 1022
DINNER **Ghillies**
894 Point Pleasant
(020) 8871 9267
DRINK **Coat & Badge**
8 Lacy Rd
(020) 8788 4900

EDGWARE ROAD
BREKKIE **Millennium**
10 Bouverie Pl
(020) 7706 4065
LUNCH **Jamuna**
38 Southwick St
(020) 7723 5056
DINNER **Patogh**
8 Crawford Pl
(020) 7262 4015
DRINK **Salt**
82 Seymour St
(020) 7402 1155

ELEPHANT&CASTLE
BREKKIE **Court Café**
38 Newington Cswy
(020) 7378 0176
LUNCH **The Lobster Pot**
3 Kennington Ln
(020) 7582 5556
DINNER **Dragon Castle**
114 Walworth St
(020) 7277 3388
DRINK **Charlie Chaplin**
26 New Kent Rd
(020) 7703 6117

EMBANKMENT
BREKKIE **Ha! Ha! Bar**
6 Villiers St
(020) 7930 1263
LUNCH **Hispaniola**
Victoria Embkt
(020) 7839 3011
DINNER **Biagio Trattoria**
17 Villiers St
(020) 7839 3633
DRINK **Gordon's**
47 Villiers St
(020) 7930 1408

EUSTON
BREKKIE **Alison's**
78 Eversholt St
(020) 7916 5485
LUNCH **Chives**
1 Woburn Wlk
(020) 7388 3479
DINNER **Chutneys**
124 Drummond St
(020) 7388 0604
DRINK **The Rocket**
120 Euston Rd
(020) 7388 0021

EUSTON SQ
BREKKIE **Rive Gauche**
20–21 Warren St
(020) 7387 8232
LUNCH **Great Nepalese**
48 Eversholt St
(020) 7388 6737
DINNER **Raavi Kebab**
125 Drummond St
(020) 7388 1780
DRINK **Jeremy Bentham**
31 University St
(020) 7387 3033

FARRINGDON
BREKKIE **Al's Bar Café**
11–13 Exmouth Mkt
(020) 7837 4821
LUNCH **St John**
26 St John St
(020) 7251 0848
DINNER **Meet**
85 Charterhouse St
(020) 7490 7490
DRINK **Betsey Trotwood**
56 Farringdon Rd
(020) 7253 4285

FINCHLEY ROAD
BREKKIE **Joe's**
3 Goldhurst Ter
(020) 7328 2295
LUNCH **Just Around...**
446 Finchley Rd
(020) 7431 3300
DINNER **Green Cottage**
9 New College Pde
(020) 7722 5305
DRINK **Duke of Hamilton**
23–25 New End
(020) 7794 0258

FINSBURY PK
BREKKIE **Banners**
21 Park Rd
(020) 8348 2930
LUNCH **La Porchetta**
147 Stroud Green Rd
(020) 7281 2892
DINNER **Hummingbird**
84 Stroud Green Rd
(020) 7263 9690
DRINK **Faltering Fullback**
19 Perth Rd
(020) 7272 5834

FULHAM BDWY
BREKKIE **Vingt Quatre**
325 Fulham Rd
(020) 7376 7224
LUNCH **1492**
404 North End Rd
(020) 7381 3810
DINNER **Wine & Kebab**
343 Fulham Rd
(020) 7352 0967
DRINK **Havana**
490 Fulham Rd
(020) 7328 1477

GLOUCESTER RD
BREKKIE **La Liaison**
130 Gloucester Rd
(020) 7370 3189
LUNCH **Jakobs**
20 Gloucester Rd
(020) 7581 9292
DINNER **Black & Blue**
105 Gloucester Rd
(020) 7244 7666
DRINK **Drayton Arms**
153 Old Brompton Rd
(020) 7835 2301

GOLDHAWK RD
BREKKIE **Adam's Café**
111 Shepherds Bush Rd
(020) 7602 2798
LUNCH **Sodere**
143 Goldhawk Rd
(020) 8811 8011
DINNER **Bush Bar & Grill**
45a Goldhawk Rd
(020) 8746 2111
DRINK **Vesbar**
15–19 Goldhawk Rd
(020) 8762 0215

GOODGE ST
BREKKIE **Italiano**
46 Goodge St
(020) 7580 9688
LUNCH **Squat & Gobble**
69 Charlotte St
(020) 7580 5338
DINNER **Archipelago**
110 Whitfield St
(020) 7637 1178
DRINK **Fitzroy Tavern**
16 Charlotte St
(020) 7580 3714

⊖ GT PORTLAND ST

BREKKIE Villandry
170 Great Portland St
(020) 7631 3131
LUNCH Annex 3
6 Little Portland St
(020) 7631 0700
DINNER Mash
19–21 Great Portland St
(020) 7637 5555
DRINK The Albany
240 Great Portland St
(020) 7387 0221

⊖ GREEN PARK

BREKKIE Mona Lisa
19 Landsdowne Row
(020) 7253 1612
LUNCH The Ritz
Piccadilly
(020) 7493 8181
DINNER Chez Gérard
31 Dover St
(020) 7499 8171
DRINK Zeta
35 Hertford St
(020) 7208 4067

⊖ HAMMERSMITH

BREKKIE Café Crema
18 The Broadway
(020) 8748 4477
LUNCH The George
28 Hammersmith Bdwy
(020) 8748 9474
DINNER The Garden
1 Shortlands
(020) 8741 1555
DRINK The Laurie Arms
238 Shepherds Bush Rd
(020) 8748 3231

⊖ HAMPSTEAD

BREKKIE Bagel Street
Oriel Pl
(020) 7431 6709
LUNCH Dim T Café
3 Heath St
(020) 7435 0024
DINNER Bacchus Taverna
37 Heath St
(020) 7435 1855
DRINK The Holly Bush
22 Holly Mount
(020) 7435 2892

⊖ HIGH ST KEN

BREKKIE Balans
187 Kensington High St
(020) 7376 0115
LUNCH Papaya Tree
209 Kensington High St
(020) 7937 2260
DINNER Cuba
11 Kensington High St
(020) 7937 4137
DRINK Jimmy's
18 Kensington Church St
(020) 7937 9988

⊖ HIGHBURY&IS

BREKKIE Workers Café
172 Upper St
(020) 7226 3973
LUNCH Bierodrome
173–174 Upper St
(020) 7226 5835
DINNER Le Mercury
140a Upper St
(020) 7354 4088
DRINK Hope & Anchor
207 Upper St
(020) 7354 1312

⊖ HOLBORN

BREKKIE Paul
296–298 High Holborn
(020) 7430 0639
LUNCH Belgo Centraal
50 Earlham St
(020) 7813 2233
DINNER My Old Dutch
132 High Holborn
(020) 7242 5200
DRINK Cittie of Yorke
22 High Holborn
(020) 7242 7670

⊖ HOLLAND PK

BREKKIE Tootsies
120 Holland Park Ave
(020) 7229 867
LUNCH The Aix
81 Holland Pk
(020) 7727 7288
DINNER Royal Tandoori
184 Holland Park Ave
(020) 7603 4778
DRINK Prince of Wales
14 Princedale Rd
(020) 7313 9321

⊖ HOLLOWAY RD

BREKKIE Café L'Arome
256 Holloway Rd
(020) 7607 5965
LUNCH Morgan M
489 Liverpool Rd
(020) 7609 3560
DINNER El Molino
379 Holloway Rd
(020) 7700 4312
DRINK Big Red
385 Holloway Rd
(020) 7609 6662

⊖ HYDE PK CORNER

BREKKIE Knightsbridge
5–6 William St
(020) 7235 4040
LUNCH Pizza on the Park
11 Knightsbridge
(020) 7235 7825
DINNER Salloos
62–64 Kinnerton St
(020) 7235 4444
DRINK Mandarin Bar
66 Knightsbridge
(020) 7235 2000

⊖ KENNINGTON

BREKKIE Parma Café
412 Kennington Rd
(020) 7787 8444
LUNCH Painted Heron
205–209 Kennington Ln
(020) 7793 8313
DINNER La Finca
185 Kennington Ln
(020) 7820 9310
DRINK Prince of Wales
Cleaver Sq
(020) 7735 9916

⊖ KENSAL GREEN

BREKKIE Nest-Café
549 Harrow Rd
(020) 8964 3953
LUNCH Manhattan Pizza
20 Station Ter
(020) 8960 4179
DINNER Paradise
19 Kilburn Ln
(020) 8969 0098
DRINK William IV
786 Harrow Rd
(020) 8969 5944

⊖ KENSINGTON

BREKKIE Frank's
3 Station Arcade
(020) 8741 4839
LUNCH Bonjour Tamarr
113 Hammersmith Rd
(020) 7603 6334
DINNER Apadana
351 Kensington High St
(020) 7603 3696
DRINK The Queen's Head
13 Brook Grn
(020) 7603 3174

⊖ KENTISH TOWN

BREKKIE Café Renoir
244 Kentish Town Rd
(020) 7284 2066
LUNCH Bengal Lancer
253 Kentish Town Rd
(020) 7485 6688
DINNER Pizza Express
187 Kentish Town Rd
(020) 7267 0101
DRINK Bull and Gate
389 Kentish Town Rd
(020) 7485 5358

⊖ KILBURN

BREKKIE Ellie's
316 Kilburn High Rd
No phone
LUNCH Cookies & Cream
321–323 Kilburn High Rd
(020) 7328 7787
DINNER Small & Beautiful
351–353 Kilburn High Rd
(020) 7604 2637
DRINK Luminaire
311 Kilburn High Rd
(020) 7372 7123

⊖ KILBURN PK

BREKKIE Little Bay
228 Belsize Rd
(020) 7372 4699
LUNCH Tasty Kebabs
39 Kilburn High Rd
(020) 7624 8414
DINNER Beirut Cellar
248 Belsize Rd
(020) 7328 3472
DRINK The Bird in Hand
12 West End Ln
(020) 7328 1477

Tube tips

KING'S CROSS
BREKKIE **Station Café**
262 Pentonville Rd
(020) 7713 7111
LUNCH **British Library**
96 Euston Rd
(020) 7412 7332
DINNER **The Other Side**
246–248 Pentonville Rd
(020) 7713 0600
DRINK **The Water Rats**
328 Grays Inn Rd
(020) 7837 7269

KNIGHTSBRIDGE
BREKKIE **Knightsbridge**
5–6 William St
(020) 7235 4040
LUNCH **Wagamama**
109–125 Knightsbridge
(020) 7235 5000
DINNER **Borshtch 'n' Tears**
45 Beauchamp Pl
(020) 7589 5003
DRINK **Mandarin Bar**
66 Knightsbridge
(020) 7235 2000

LADBROKE GROVE
BREKKIE **Uncle's**
305 Portobello Rd
(020) 8962 0090
LUNCH **Hummingbird Café**
133 Portobello Rd
(020) 7229 6446
DINNER **Osteria Basilico**
29 Kensington Park Rd
(020) 7324 4455
DRINK **The Pelican**
140–145 All Saints' Rd
(020) 7792 3682

LAMBETH NORTH
BREKKIE **Perdoni's**
20 Kennington High Rd
(020) 7253 1612
LUNCH **Cubana**
48 Lower Marsh
(020) 7928 8778
DINNER **Inshoku**
23–24 Lower Marsh
(020) 7928 2311
DRINK **Three Stags**
67 Kennington Rd
(020) 7928 5974

LATIMER RD
BREKKIE **Tea's Me**
129a Ladbroke Gve
(020) 7792 5577
LUNCH **Notting Grill**
123a Clarendon Rd
(020) 7229 1500
DINNER **The Station**
41 Bramley Rd
(020) 7229 1111
DRINK **Kenilworth Castle**
104 St Ann's Rd
(020) 7727 0656

LEICESTER SQ
BREKKIE **The Stockpot**
38 Panton St
(020) 7839 5142
LUNCH **Ikkyusan**
39 Gerrard St
(020) 7434 0899
DINNER **Gili Gulu**
50–52 Monmouth St
(020) 7379 6888
DRINK **White Horse**
45 Rupert St
(020) 7437 5745

LIVERPOOL ST
BREKKIE **Beigel Bakery**
159 Brick Ln
(020) 7729 0616
LUNCH **The Light**
233 Shoreditch High St
(020) 7247 8989
DINNER **Tatsuso**
32 Broadgate Circle
(020) 7638 5863
DRINK **The Gun**
54 Brushfield St
(020) 7247 7988

LONDON BRIDGE
BREKKIE **Borough Café**
11 Park St
(020) 7407 5048
LUNCH **Anchor Bankside**
34 Park St
(020) 7407 1577
DINNER **Menier Theatre**
53 Southwark St
(020) 7378 1712
DRINK **Vinopolis**
London Bridge, Bankside
(020) 7940 8322

MAIDA VALE
BREKKIE **Raoul's**
10 Clifton Rd
(020) 7289 6649
LUNCH **Ben's Thai**
93 Warrington Crs
(020) 7266 3134
DINNER **Red Pepper**
8 Formosa St
(020) 7266 2708
DRINK **The Warrington**
93 Warrington Crs
(020) 7263 7234

MANSION HOUSE
BREKKIE **Chapters Deli**
70 Cannon St
(020) 7248 3034
LUNCH **Fifteen 05**
All Hallows Ln
(020) 7283 1505
DINNER **Silks & Spice**
11 Queen Victoria St
(020) 7248 7878
DRINK **Ye Olde Watling**
29 Watling St
(020) 7653 9971

MARBLE ARCH
BREKKIE **Mosco's Café**
26 North Audley St
(020) 7493 0090
LUNCH **Selfridges**
400 Oxford St
(0870) 837 7377
DINNER **Maroush**
21 Edgware Rd
(020) 7723 0773
DRINK **Mason's Arms**
51 Berkely St
(020) 7723 2131

MARYLEBONE
BREKKIE **Patisserie Valerie**
105 Marylebone High St
(020) 7935 6240
LUNCH **Yakitoria**
25 Sheldon Sq
(020) 3214 3000
DINNER **The Providores**
109 Marylebone High St
(020) 7935 6175
DRINK **Prince Regent**
71 Marylebone High St
(020) 7467 3811

MILE END
BREKKIE **Gardiner's**
630 Mile End Rd
(020) 8980 3984
LUNCH **Matsu**
558 Mile End Rd
(020) 8983 3528
DINNER **Britannia Fish Bar**
101 Grove Rd
(020) 8983 3414
DRINK **The Palm Tree**
Haverfield Rd
No phone

MONUMENT
BREKKIE **Café**
20 Little Britain
(020) 755 4489
LUNCH **TK's**
31 Lovat Ln
(020) 7220 7613
DINNER **Prism**
17 Leadenhall St
(020) 7256 3888
DRINK **City Tup**
66 Gersham St
(020) 7606 8176

MOORGATE
BREKKIE **Smiths**
77 Charterhouse St
(020) 7251 7950
LUNCH **Nylon**
11 Addle St
(020) 7600 7771
DINNER **Sushi & Soza**
Moorgate Station
(020) 7638 3866
DRINK **The Globe**
Moorgate
(020) 7786 9241

MORN CRES
BREKKIE **Bites**
46 Mornington Crs
(020) 7383 3484
LUNCH **El Parador**
245 Eversholt St
(020) 7387 2789
DINNER **Asakusa**
265 Eversholt St
(020) 7388 8533
DRINK **The Victoria**
2 Mornington Ter
(020) 7387 3804

⊖ NEW CROSS

BREKKIE Café Crema
306 New Cross Rd
(020) 8320 2317
LUNCH Noodle King
36 Deptford Bdwy
(020) 8692 9633
DINNER Alanya
164 New Cross Rd
(020) 7639 3751
DRINK Goldsmith's Tavern
316 New Cross Rd
(020) 8692 3193

⊖ N GREENWICH

BREKKIE Holiday Inn
Bugsby Way
(0870) 400 9670
LUNCH Memsaheb
65–67 Amsterdam Rd
(020) 7538 3008
DINNER The Gun
27 Cold Harbour
(020) 7515 5222
DRINK Pilot Inn
68 River Way
(020) 8858 5910

⊖ NOTTING HILL

BREKKIE Dakota
127 Ledbury Rd
(020) 7792 9191
LUNCH The Ark
122 Palace Gdns Ter
(020) 7229 4024
DINNER Café Mandola
141 Westbourne Gv
(020) 7229 4734
DRINK Sun in Splendour
7 Portobello Rd
(020) 7313 9331

⊖ OLD ST

BREKKIE Cantaloupe
35 Charlotte Rd
(020) 7613 4411
LUNCH La Scala
74 Luke St
(020) 7613 1230
DINNER Yelo
8–9 Hoxton Sq
(020) 7729 4626
DRINK Wenlock Arms
26 Wenlock St
(020) 7608 3408

⊖ OVAL

BREKKIE Oval Café
312 Kennington Pk Rd
(020) 7735 4603
LUNCH The Timegad
5 Brixton Station Rd
(020) 7737 1809
DINNER Lavender
171 Lavender Hl
(020) 7978 5242
DRINK Fentiman Arms
64 Fentiman Rd
(020) 7793 9796

⊖ OXFORD CIRCUS

BREKKIE Bar Chocolate
27 D'Arblay St
(020) 7287 2923
LUNCH Léon
36 Gt Marlborough St
(020) 7437 5280
DINNER Kerala
15 Great Castle St
(020) 7580 2125
DRINK Marlborough Head
24 North Audley St
(020) 7629 5981

⊖ PADDINGTON

BREKKIE Caffé Nero
Paddington Station
(020) 7402 0417
LUNCH Indus Delta
135 Praed St
(020) 7723 3191
DINNER Los Remos
38 Southwick St
(020) 7706 1870
DRINK Steam
1 Eastbourne Ter
(020) 7850 0555

⊖ PARSON'S GRN

BREKKIE Tootsies
177 New Kings Rd
(020) 7736 4023
LUNCH The Durrell
704 Fulham Rd
(020) 7736 3014
DINNER Pappa & Ciccia
105 Munster Rd
(020) 7384 1884
DRINK The White Horse
1–3 Parson's Grn
(020) 7736 2115

⊖ PICCADILLY CIRC

BREKKIE The Stockpot
38 Panton St
(020) 7839 5142
LUNCH New Piccadilly
8 Denman St
(020) 7437 8530
DINNER Momo
25 Heddon St
(020) 7434 4040
DRINK St James Tavern
45 Great Windmill St
(020) 7437 5009

⊖ PIMLICO

BREKKIE Relish
8 John Islip St
(020) 7828 0628
LUNCH Grumbles
35 Churlton St
(020) 7834 0149
DINNER Top Curry Centre
3 Lupus St
(020) 7821 7572
DRINK Elusive Camel
27 Gillingham St
(020) 7233 9004

⊖ PUTNEY

BREKKIE River Café
1a Station Approach
(020) 7736 6296
LUNCH Kazbar
24 Putney High St
(020) 8780 0929
DINNER La Mancha
32 Putney High St
(020) 8780 1022
DRINK Half Moon
93 Lower Richmond Rd
(020) 8780 9383

⊖ QUEEN'S PK

BREKKIE Hugo's
25 Lonsdale Rd
(020) 7372 1232
LUNCH The Sundarban
77 Salusbury Rd
(020) 7624 8852
DINNER Penk's
79 Salusbury Rd
(020) 7736 2115
DRINK The Greyhound
50–52 Salusbury Rd
(020) 7328 3286

⊖ QUEENSWAY

BREKKIE Café Fresco
25 Westbourne Grv
(020) 7221 2355
LUNCH Khan's
13–15 Westbourne Grv
(020) 7727 5420
DINNER Royal China
13 Queensway
(020) 7221 2535
DRINK The King's Head
33 Moscow Rd
(020) 7229 4233

⊖ RAYNERS LANE

BREKKIE Imperial Café
236 Imperial Dr
(020) 8868 1189
LUNCH Papaya
15 Village Way East
(020) 8866 5582
DINNER Silver Dollar
230 Imperial Dr
(020) 8866 9226
DRINK The Village Inn
402–408 Rayner's Ln
(020) 8868 8551

⊖ REGENT'S PK

BREKKIE Villandry
170 Great Portland St
(020) 7631 3131
LUNCH Honest Sausage
Regent's Park
(020) 7224 3872
DINNER Getti
42 Marylebone High St
(020) 7486 3753
DRINK Dover Castle
43 Weymouth Mws
(020) 7580 4412

⊖ ROTHERHITHE

BREKKIE Spud-u-Like
Redriff Rd
(020) 7252 3071
LUNCH Fish King
11 Plough Way
(020) 8980 1042
DINNER The Angel
101 Bermondsey Wall
(020) 7237 3608
DRINK Spice Island
163 Rotherhithe St
(020) 7394 7108

Tube tips

🚇 ROYAL OAK
BREKKIE **Café Bijou**
1 Sutherland Ave
(020) 7432 8782
LUNCH **The Westbourne**
101 Westbourne Pk Vls
(020) 7221 1332
DINNER **Anthony's**
54 Porchester Rd
(020) 7243 8743
DRINK **Royal Oak**
88 Bishops Bridge Rd
(020) 7229 2886

🚇 RUSSELL SQ
BREKKIE **Garden Café**
Russell Sq
No phone
LUNCH **Busaba Eathai**
22 Store St
(020) 7299 7900
DINNER **Hare & Tortoise**
15–17 Brunswick Ctr
(020) 7278 9799
DRINK **Marquis Cornwallis**
36 Marchmont St
(020) 7923 5960

🚇 SOUTHWARK
BREKKIE **The Table**
85 Southwark St
(020) 7401 2760
LUNCH **Meson Don Felipe**
53 The Cut
(020) 7928 3237
DINNER **Anchor & Hope**
36 The Cut
(020) 7928 9898
DRINK **The Ring**
72 Blackfriars Rd
(020) 7928 2589

🚇 ST JAMES'S PK
BREKKIE **Broadway Café**
16 Broadway
(020) 7222 2646
LUNCH **Inn the Park**
St James's Pk
(020) 7451 9999
DINNER **The Phoenix**
14 Palace St
(020) 7834 3547
DRINK **Two Chairmen**
39 Dartmouth St
(020) 7222 8694

🚇 ST JOHN'S WOOD
BREKKIE **Café Rouge**
St John's Wood High St
(020) 7722 8366
LUNCH **Caffe Uno**
St John's Wood High St
(020) 7722 0400
DINNER **L'Aventure**
3 Blenheim Ter
(020) 7624 6232
DRINK **The Salt House**
63 Abbey Rd
(020) 7328 6626

🚇 ST PAUL'S
BREKKIE **Café**
20 Little Britain
(020) 7355 4489
LUNCH **The Refectory**
St Paul's Churchyard
(020) 7246 8358
DINNER **Just the Bridge**
1 Paul's Wlk
(020) 7236 0000
DRINK **Balls Brothers**
6–8 Cheapside
(020) 7248 2708

🚇 STAMFORD BRK
BREKKIE **The Ritz**
340a King St
(020) 8748 7517
LUNCH **Yellow River Café**
12 Chiswick High St
(020) 8987 9791
DINNER **Anarkali**
303 King St
(020) 8748 1760
DRINK **The Hart**
383 King St
(020) 8748 6076

🚇 STEPNEY GRN
BREKKIE **Mr G's Café**
222 Mile End Rd
(020) 7790 2724
LUNCH **Pride of Asia**
207 Mile End Rd
(020) 7780 9321
DINNER **Taja**
199 Whitechapel Rd
(020) 7247 3866
DRINK **New Globe**
359 Mile End Project
(020) 8981 2800

🚇 STOCKWELL
BREKKIE **Stockwell Café**
197 Stockwell Rd
(020) 7274 1724
LUNCH **Rebato's**
169 South Lambeth Rd
(020) 7735 6388
DINNER **Al Montanha**
71 Stockwell Rd
(020) 7737 5961
DRINK **Circle Bar**
348 Clapham Rd
(020) 7622 3683

🚇 SURREY QUAYS
BREKKIE **Hubbub**
269 Westferry Rd
(020) 7515 5577
LUNCH **GB Kebabs**
152 Lower Rd
(020) 7237 8064
DINNER **The Angel**
101 Bermondsey Wall
(020) 7237 3608
DRINK **Spice Island**
163 Rotherhithe St
(020) 7394 7108

🚇 SWISS COTTAGE
BREKKIE **Café Arch**
17 Northways Pde
(020) 7483 4089
LUNCH **Singapore Garden**
83 Fairfax Rd
(020) 7328 5314
DINNER **Benihana**
100 Avenue Rd
(020) 7586 9508
DRINK **Elbow Rooms**
135 Finchley Rd
(020) 7586 9888

🚇 TEMPLE
BREKKIE **Pret a Manger**
421 The Strand
(020) 7240 5900
LUNCH **Leith's**
113 Chancery Ln
(020) 7278 1234
DINNER **The Admiralty**
150 The Strand
(020) 7845 4646
DRINK **Lyceum Tavern**
345 The Strand
(020) 7836 7155

🚇 TOTT CT RD
BREKKIE **Apostrophe**
216 Tottenham Ct Rd
(020) 7436 6688
LUNCH **Assa**
53 St Giles High St
(020) 7240 8256
DINNER **Rasa**
5 Rathbone St
(020) 7637 0222
DRINK **Bradley's**
42 Hanway St
(020) 7636 0359

🚇 TOWER HILL
BREKKIE **Tower Patisserie**
St Katharine's Dock
(020) 7481 1464
LUNCH **La Lanterna**
6 Mill St
(020) 7252 3054
DINNER **Aquarium**
St Katharine's Dock
(020) 7480 6116
DRINK **Dickens Inn**
St Katharine's Dock
(020) 7488 2208

🚇 TUFNELL PK
BREKKIE **Rustique**
142 Fortess Rd
(020) 7692 5590
LUNCH **Lord Palmerston**
33 Dartmouth Park Hill
(020) 7485 1578
DINNER **Lalibela**
137 Fortess Rd
(020) 7284 0600
DRINK **Junction Tavern**
101 Fortess Rd
(020) 7485 9200

🚇 TURNHAM GRN
BREKKIE **La Mirage**
309 Chiswick High Rd
(020) 8994 1661
LUNCH **Dumela**
42 Devonshire Rd
(020) 8742 3149
DINNER **West Kebab**
196 Chiswick High Rd
(020) 8742 3617
DRINK **George IV**
185 Chiswick High Rd
(020) 8994 4624

⊖ VAUXHALL

BREKKIE Pavilion Café
New Covent Gdn Mkt
(020) 8466 7233
LUNCH Bonnington Café
11 Vauxhall Grv
(020) 7820 7466
DINNER Lavender
112 Vauxhall Wlk
(020) 7735 4440
DRINK Royal Vauxhall
372 Kennington Ln
(020) 7582 0833

⊖ VICTORIA

BREKKIE Alpino Snack Bar
8 Elizabeth St
(020) 7730 8400
LUNCH The Cardinal
23 Francis St
(020) 7834 7260
DINNER Kazan
93 Wilton Rd
(020) 7233 7100
DRINK The Shakespeare
99 Buckingham Palace Rd
(020) 7828 4913

⊖ WAPPING

BREKKIE The Wall
61 Wapping Wall
(020) 7709 7887
LUNCH Riverview Chinese
16 New Crane Pl
(020) 7480 6026
DINNER Wapping Project
Wapping Wall
(020) 7608 2080
DRINK The Mayflower
117 Rotherhithe St
(020) 7237 4088

⊖ WARREN ST

BREKKIE Rive Gauche
20–21 Warren St
(020) 7387 8232
LUNCH Roka
37 Charlotte St
(020) 7580 6464
DINNER Dim T
32 Charlotte St
(020) 7637 1122
DRINK The One Tun
58–60 Goodge St
(020) 7209 4105

⊖ WATERLOO

BREKKIE Marie's Café
90 Lower Marsh
(020) 7928 1050
LUNCH Konditor & Cook
10 Stoney St
(020) 7404 5100
DINNER Ned's Noodle Box
3 Belvedere Rd
(020) 7593 0077
DRINK The White Hart
29 Cornwall Rd
(020) 7401 7151

⊖ WARWICK AV

BREKKIE Lospuntino
18 Formosa St
(020) 7266 2043
LUNCH Red Pepper
8 Formosa St
(020) 7266 2708
DINNER Prince Alfred
5a Formosa St
(020) 7286 3287
DRINK The Bridge House
13 Westbourne Ter Rd
(020) 7432 1361

⊖ WEMBLEY PK

BREKKIE Moulin Grill
139 Wembley Park Dr
(020) 8902 1799
LUNCH The Ugly Duckling
121 Wembley Park Dr
(020) 8900 1157
DINNER New Kabana
43 Blackbird Hl
(020) 8200 7094
DRINK The Torch
1–5 Bridge Rd
(020) 8904 5794

⊖ W BROMPTON

BREKKIE Troubadour
265 Old Brompton Rd
(020) 7370 1434
LUNCH The Grill
2–4 Lillie Rd
(020) 7381 4339
DINNER Atlas
16 Seagrave Rd
(020) 7385 9129
DRINK Balans West
239 Old Brompton Rd
(020) 7244 8838

⊖ W HAMPSTEAD

BREKKIE Mr Gingham
112 West End Ln
(020) 7253 1612
LUNCH Wet Fish Café
242 West End Ln
(020) 7433 9222
DINNER The Gallery
190 Broadhurst Gdns
(020) 7625 9184
DRINK Lately's
175 West End Ln
(020) 7625 6474

⊖ W KENSINGTON

BREKKIE Continente
62 North End Rd
(020) 7603 6311
LUNCH Veggie Vegan
222 North End Rd
(020) 7381 2322
DINNER Ta Krai
100 North End Rd
(020) 7386 5375
DRINK Fox Rattle & Hum
3 North End Crs
(020) 7603 7006

⊖ WESTBOURNE PK

BREKKIE Mike's Café
12 Blenheim Crs
(020) 7229 3757
LUNCH The Cedar
65 Fernhead Rd
(020) 8964 2011
DINNER The Cow
89 Westbourne Pk Rd
(020) 7221 0021
DRINK Babushka
41 Tavistock Crs
(020) 7727 9250

⊖ WESTMINSTER

BREKKIE Caffé Nero
1–2 Bridge St
(020) 7925 0781
LUNCH The Footstool
Smith Sq
(020) 7222 2779
DINNER Cinnamon Club
30–32 Great Smith St
(020) 7222 2555
DRINK The Red Lion
48 Parliament St
(020) 7930 5826

⊖ WHITE CITY

BREKKIE Sonia's Café
308 Latimer Rd
(020) 8746 8956
LUNCH The Lunch Box
235 Wood Ln
(020) 8746 2365
DINNER Fatima
253 Wood Ln
(020) 8749 1323
DRINK Springbok
51 South Africa Rd
(020) 8743 8476

⊖ WHITECHAPEL

BREKKIE Mr G's Café
222 Mile End Rd
(020) 7790 2724
LUNCH Nando's
19 Mile End Rd
(020) 7729 5783
DINNER Clifton Restaurant
1 Whitechapel Rd
(020) 7377 5533
DRINK Indo
133 Whitechapel Rd
(020) 7247 4826

⊖ WILLESDEN GRN

BREKKIE S & B
351 Kilburn High Rd
(020) 7328 2637
LUNCH CoCo's Tapas
41–43 High Rd
(020) 8830 1638
DINNER Shish
2–6 Station Pde
(020) 8208 9292
DRINK Ned Kelly's
305 High St
(020) 8459 3020

⊖ WOOD GREEN

BREKKIE Villa del Flori
Shopping City
(020) 8365 8046
LUNCH Vrisaki
73 Myddleton Rd
(020) 8889 8760
DINNER Mosaica
Clarendon Rd
(020) 8889 2400
DRINK The Nelson
232–234 High Rd
(020) 1984 4791

Index

Index

Index